metrix

TEST PREPARATION

MCA

Success Strategies Grade 6 Reading

Dear Future Exam Success Story

First of all, **THANK YOU** for purchasing Mometrix study materials!

Second, congratulations! You are one of the few determined test-takers who are committed to doing whatever it takes to excel on your exam. **You have come to the right place.** We developed these study materials with one goal in mind: to deliver you the information you need in a format that's concise and easy to use.

In addition to optimizing your guide for the content of the test, we've outlined our recommended steps for breaking down the preparation process into small, attainable goals so you can make sure you stay on track.

We've also analyzed the entire test-taking process, identifying the most common pitfalls and showing how you can overcome them and be ready for any curveball the test throws you.

Standardized testing is one of the biggest obstacles on your road to success, which only increases the importance of doing well in the high-pressure, high-stakes environment of test day. Your results on this test could have a significant impact on your future, and this guide provides the information and practical advice to help you achieve your full potential on test day.

Your success is our success

We would love to hear from you! If you would like to share the story of your exam success or if you have any questions or comments in regard to our products, please contact us at **800-673-8175** or **support@mometrix.com**.

Thanks again for your business and we wish you continued success!

Sincerely,
The Mometrix Test Preparation Team

Written and edited by the Mometrix Test Preparation Team
Printed in the United States of America

Table of Contents

Introduction

Thank you for purchasing this resource! You have made the choice to prepare yourself for a test that could have a huge impact on your future, and this guide is designed to help you be fully ready for test day. Obviously, it's important to have a solid understanding of the test material, but you also need to be prepared for the unique environment and stressors of the test, so that you can perform to the best of your abilities.

For this purpose, the first section that appears in this guide is the **Success Strategies**. We've devoted countless hours to meticulously researching what works and what doesn't, and we've boiled down our findings to the most impactful steps you can take to improve your performance on the test. We start at the beginning with study planning and move through the preparation process, all the way to the testing strategies that will help you get the most out of what you know when you're finally sitting in front of the test.

We recommend that you start preparing for your test as far in advance as possible. However, if you've bought this guide as a last-minute study resource and only have a few days before your test, we recommend that you skip over the first two Success Strategies since they address a long-term study plan.

If you struggle with **test anxiety**, we strongly encourage you to check out our recommendations for how you can overcome it. Test anxiety is a formidable foe, but it can be beaten, and we want to make sure you have the tools you need to defeat it.

Strategy #1 – Plan Big, Study Small

There's a lot riding on your performance. If you want to ace this test, you're going to need to keep your skills sharp and the material fresh in your mind. You need a plan that lets you review everything you need to know while still fitting in your schedule. We'll break this strategy down into three categories.

Information Organization

Start with the information you already have: the official test outline. From this, you can make a complete list of all the concepts you need to cover before the test. Organize these concepts into groups that can be studied together, and create a list of any related vocabulary you need to learn so you can brush up on any difficult terms. You'll want to keep this vocabulary list handy once you actually start studying since you may need to add to it along the way.

Time Management

Once you have your set of study concepts, decide how to spread them out over the time you have left before the test. Break your study plan into small, clear goals so you have a manageable task for each day and know exactly what you're doing. Then just focus on one small step at a time. When you manage your time this way, you don't need to spend hours at a time studying. Studying a small block of content for a short period each day helps you retain information better and avoid stressing over how much you have left to do. You can relax knowing that you have a plan to cover everything in time. In order for this strategy to be effective though, you have to start studying early and stick to your schedule. Avoid the exhaustion and futility that comes from last-minute cramming!

Study Environment

The environment you study in has a big impact on your learning. Studying in a coffee shop, while probably more enjoyable, is not likely to be as fruitful as studying in a quiet room. It's important to keep distractions to a minimum. You're only planning to study for a short block of time, so make the most of it. Don't pause to check your phone or get up to find a snack. It's also important to **avoid multitasking**. Research has consistently shown that multitasking will make your studying dramatically less effective. Your study area should also be comfortable and well-lit so you don't have the distraction of straining your eyes or sitting on an uncomfortable chair.

The time of day you study is also important. You want to be rested and alert. Don't wait until just before bedtime. Study when you'll be most likely to comprehend and remember. Even better, if you know what time of day your test will be, set that time aside for study. That way your brain will be used to working on that subject at that specific time and you'll have a better chance of recalling information.

Finally, it can be helpful to team up with others who are studying for the same test. Your actual studying should be done in as isolated an environment as possible, but the work of organizing the information and setting up the study plan can be divided up. In between study sessions, you can discuss with your teammates the concepts that you're all studying and quiz each other on the details. Just be sure that your teammates are as serious about the test as you are. If you find that your study time is being replaced with social time, you might need to find a new team.

Strategy #2 – Make Your Studying Count

You're devoting a lot of time and effort to preparing for this test, so you want to be absolutely certain it will pay off. This means doing more than just reading the content and hoping you can remember it on test day. It's important to make every minute of study count. There are two main areas you can focus on to make your studying count.

Retention

It doesn't matter how much time you study if you can't remember the material. You need to make sure you are retaining the concepts. To check your retention of the information you're learning, try recalling it at later times with minimal prompting. Try carrying around flashcards and glance at one or two from time to time or ask a friend who's also studying for the test to quiz you.

To enhance your retention, look for ways to put the information into practice so that you can apply it rather than simply recalling it. If you're using the information in practical ways, it will be much easier to remember. Similarly, it helps to solidify a concept in your mind if you're not only reading it to yourself but also explaining it to someone else. Ask a friend to let you teach them about a concept you're a little shaky on (or speak aloud to an imaginary audience if necessary). As you try to summarize, define, give examples, and answer your friend's questions, you'll understand the concepts better and they will stay with you longer. Finally, step back for a big picture view and ask yourself how each piece of information fits with the whole subject. When you link the different concepts together and see them working together as a whole, it's easier to remember the individual components.

Finally, practice showing your work on any multi-step problems, even if you're just studying. Writing out each step you take to solve a problem will help solidify the process in your mind, and you'll be more likely to remember it during the test.

Modality

Modality simply refers to the means or method by which you study. Choosing a study modality that fits your own individual learning style is crucial. No two people learn best in exactly the same way, so it's important to know your strengths and use them to your advantage.

For example, if you learn best by visualization, focus on visualizing a concept in your mind and draw an image or a diagram. Try color-coding your notes, illustrating them, or creating symbols that will trigger your mind to recall a learned concept. If you learn best by hearing or discussing information, find a study partner who learns the same way or read aloud to yourself. Think about how to put the information in your own words. Imagine that you are giving a lecture on the topic and record yourself so you can listen to it later.

For any learning style, flashcards can be helpful. Organize the information so you can take advantage of spare moments to review. Underline key words or phrases. Use different colors for different categories. Mnemonic devices (such as creating a short list in which every item starts with the same letter) can also help with retention. Find what works best for you and use it to store the information in your mind most effectively and easily.

Strategy #3 – Practice the Right Way

Your success on test day depends not only on how many hours you put into preparing, but also on whether you prepared the right way. It's good to check along the way to see if your studying is paying off. One of the most effective ways to do this is by taking practice tests to evaluate your progress. Practice tests are useful because they show exactly where you need to improve. Every time you take a practice test, pay special attention to these three groups of questions:

- The questions you got wrong
- The questions you had to guess on, even if you guessed right
- The questions you found difficult or slow to work through

This will show you exactly what your weak areas are, and where you need to devote more study time. Ask yourself why each of these questions gave you trouble. Was it because you didn't understand the material? Was it because you didn't remember the vocabulary? Do you need more repetitions on this type of question to build speed and confidence? Dig into those questions and figure out how you can strengthen your weak areas as you go back to review the material.

Additionally, many practice tests have a section explaining the answer choices. It can be tempting to read the explanation and think that you now have a good understanding of the concept. However, an explanation likely only covers part of the question's broader context. Even if the explanation makes perfect sense, **go back and investigate** every concept related to the question until you're positive you have a thorough understanding.

As you go along, keep in mind that the practice test is just that: practice. Memorizing these questions and answers will not be very helpful on the actual test because it is unlikely to have any of the same exact questions. If you only know the right answers to the sample questions, you won't be prepared for the real thing. **Study the concepts** until you understand them fully, and then you'll be able to answer any question that shows up on the test.

It's important to wait on the practice tests until you're ready. If you take a test on your first day of study, you may be overwhelmed by the amount of material covered and how much you need to learn. Work up to it gradually.

On test day, you'll need to be prepared for answering questions, managing your time, and using the test-taking strategies you've learned. It's a lot to balance, like a mental marathon that will have a big impact on your future. Like training for a marathon, you'll need to start slowly and work your way up. When test day arrives, you'll be ready.

Start with the strategies you've read in the first two Success Strategies—plan your course and study in the way that works best for you. If you have time, consider using multiple study resources to get different approaches to the same concepts. It can be helpful to see difficult concepts from more than one angle. Then find a good source for practice tests. Many times, the test website will suggest potential study resources or provide sample tests.

Practice Test Strategy

If you're able to find at least three practice tests, we recommend this strategy:

Untimed and Open-Book Practice

Take the first test with no time constraints and with your notes and study guide handy. Take your time and focus on applying the strategies you've learned.

Timed and Open-Book Practice

Take the second practice test open-book as well, but set a timer and practice pacing yourself to finish in time.

Timed and Closed-Book Practice

Take any other practice tests as if it were test day. Set a timer and put away your study materials. Sit at a table or desk in a quiet room, imagine yourself at the testing center, and answer questions as quickly and accurately as possible.

Keep repeating timed and closed-book tests on a regular basis until you run out of practice tests or it's time for the actual test. Your mind will be ready for the schedule and stress of test day, and you'll be able to focus on recalling the material you've learned.

Strategy #4 – Pace Yourself

Once you're fully prepared for the material on the test, your biggest challenge on test day will be managing your time. Just knowing that the clock is ticking can make you panic even if you have plenty of time left. Work on pacing yourself so you can build confidence against the time constraints of the exam. Pacing is a difficult skill to master, especially in a high-pressure environment, so **practice is vital**.

Set time expectations for your pace based on how much time is available. For example, if a section has 60 questions and the time limit is 30 minutes, you know you have to average 30 seconds or less per question in order to answer them all. Although 30 seconds is the hard limit, set 25 seconds per question as your goal, so you reserve extra time to spend on harder questions. When you budget extra time for the harder questions, you no longer have any reason to stress when those questions take longer to answer.

Don't let this time expectation distract you from working through the test at a calm, steady pace, but keep it in mind so you don't spend too much time on any one question. Recognize that taking extra time on one question you don't understand may keep you from answering two that you do understand later in the test. If your time limit for a question is up and you're still not sure of the answer, mark it and move on, and come back to it later if the time and the test format allow. If the testing format doesn't allow you to return to earlier questions, just make an educated guess; then put it out of your mind and move on.

On the easier questions, be careful not to rush. It may seem wise to hurry through them so you have more time for the challenging ones, but it's not worth missing one if you know the concept and just didn't take the time to read the question fully. Work efficiently but make sure you understand the question and have looked at all of the answer choices, since more than one may seem right at first.

Even if you're paying attention to the time, you may find yourself a little behind at some point. You should speed up to get back on track, but do so wisely. Don't panic; just take a few seconds less on each question until you're caught up. Don't guess without thinking, but do look through the answer choices and eliminate any you know are wrong. If you can get down to two choices, it is often worthwhile to guess from those. Once you've chosen an answer, move on and don't dwell on any that you skipped or had to hurry through. If a question was taking too long, chances are it was one of the harder ones, so you weren't as likely to get it right anyway.

On the other hand, if you find yourself getting ahead of schedule, it may be beneficial to slow down a little. The more quickly you work, the more likely you are to make a careless mistake that will affect your score. You've budgeted time for each question, so don't be afraid to spend that time. Practice an efficient but careful pace to get the most out of the time you have.

Test-Taking Strategies

This section contains a list of test-taking strategies that you may find helpful as you work through the test. By taking what you know and applying logical thought, you can maximize your chances of answering any question correctly!

It is very important to realize that every question is different and every person is different: no single strategy will work on every question, and no single strategy will work for every person. That's why we've included all of them here, so you can try them out and determine which ones work best for different types of questions and which ones work best for you.

Question Strategies

✓ Read Carefully

Read the question and the answer choices carefully. Don't miss the question because you misread the terms. You have plenty of time to read each question thoroughly and make sure you understand what is being asked. Yet a happy medium must be attained, so don't waste too much time. You must read carefully and efficiently.

✓ Contextual Clues

Look for contextual clues. If the question includes a word you are not familiar with, look at the immediate context for some indication of what the word might mean. Contextual clues can often give you all the information you need to decipher the meaning of an unfamiliar word. Even if you can't determine the meaning, you may be able to narrow down the possibilities enough to make a solid guess at the answer to the question.

✓ Prefixes

If you're having trouble with a word in the question or answer choices, try dissecting it. Take advantage of every clue that the word might include. Prefixes can be a huge help. Usually, they allow you to determine a basic meaning. *Pre-* means before, *post-* means after, *pro-* is positive, *de-* is negative. From prefixes, you can get an idea of the general meaning of the word and try to put it into context.

✓ Hedge Words

Watch out for critical hedge words, such as *likely, may, can, often, almost, mostly, usually, generally, rarely*, and *sometimes*. Question writers insert these hedge phrases to cover every possibility. Often an answer choice will be wrong simply because it leaves no room for exception. Be on guard for answer choices that have definitive words such as *exactly* and *always*.

✓ Switchback Words

Stay alert for *switchbacks*. These are the words and phrases frequently used to alert you to shifts in thought. The most common switchback words are *but, although*, and *however*. Others include *nevertheless, on the other hand, even though, while, in spite of, despite*, and *regardless of*. Switchback words are important to catch because they can change the direction of the question or an answer choice.

✓ Face Value

When in doubt, use common sense. Accept the situation in the problem at face value. Don't read too much into it. These problems will not require you to make wild assumptions. If you have to go beyond creativity and warp time or space in order to have an answer choice fit the question, then you should move on and consider the other answer choices. These are normal problems rooted in reality. The applicable relationship or explanation may not be readily apparent, but it is there for you to figure out. Use your common sense to interpret anything that isn't clear.

Answer Choice Strategies

✓ Answer Selection

The most thorough way to pick an answer choice is to identify and eliminate wrong answers until only one is left, then confirm it is the correct answer. Sometimes an answer choice may immediately seem right, but be careful. The test writers will usually put more than one reasonable answer choice on each question, so take a second to read all of them and make sure that the other choices are not equally obvious. As long as you have time left, it is better to read every answer choice than to pick the first one that looks right without checking the others.

✓ Answer Choice Families

An answer choice family consists of two (in rare cases, three) answer choices that are very similar in construction and cannot all be true at the same time. If you see two answer choices that are direct opposites or parallels, one of them is usually the correct answer. For instance, if one answer choice says that quantity *x* increases and another either says that quantity *x* decreases (opposite) or says that quantity *y* increases (parallel), then those answer choices would fall into the same family. An answer choice that doesn't match the construction of the answer choice family is more likely to be incorrect. Most questions will not have answer choice families, but when they do appear, you should be prepared to recognize them.

✓ Eliminate Answers

Eliminate answer choices as soon as you realize they are wrong, but make sure you consider all possibilities. If you are eliminating answer choices and realize that the last one you are left with is also wrong, don't panic. Start over and consider each choice again. There may be something you missed the first time that you will realize on the second pass.

✓ Avoid Fact Traps

Don't be distracted by an answer choice that is factually true but doesn't answer the question. You are looking for the choice that answers the question. Stay focused on what the question is asking for so you don't accidentally pick an answer that is true but incorrect. Always go back to the question and make sure the answer choice you've selected actually answers the question and is not merely a true statement.

✓ Extreme Statements

In general, you should avoid answers that put forth extreme actions as standard practice or proclaim controversial ideas as established fact. An answer choice that states the "process should be used in certain situations, if…" is much more likely to be correct than one that states the "process should be discontinued completely." The first is a calm rational statement and doesn't even make a definitive, uncompromising stance, using a hedge word *if* to provide wiggle room, whereas the second choice is far more extreme.

⊘ Benchmark

As you read through the answer choices and you come across one that seems to answer the question well, mentally select that answer choice. This is not your final answer, but it's the one that will help you evaluate the other answer choices. The one that you selected is your benchmark or standard for judging each of the other answer choices. Every other answer choice must be compared to your benchmark. That choice is correct until proven otherwise by another answer choice beating it. If you find a better answer, then that one becomes your new benchmark. Once you've decided that no other choice answers the question as well as your benchmark, you have your final answer.

⊘ Predict the Answer

Before you even start looking at the answer choices, it is often best to try to predict the answer. When you come up with the answer on your own, it is easier to avoid distractions and traps because you will know exactly what to look for. The right answer choice is unlikely to be word-for-word what you came up with, but it should be a close match. Even if you are confident that you have the right answer, you should still take the time to read each option before moving on.

General Strategies

⊘ Tough Questions

If you are stumped on a problem or it appears too hard or too difficult, don't waste time. Move on! Remember though, if you can quickly check for obviously incorrect answer choices, your chances of guessing correctly are greatly improved. Before you completely give up, at least try to knock out a couple of possible answers. Eliminate what you can and then guess at the remaining answer choices before moving on.

⊘ Check Your Work

Since you will probably not know every term listed and the answer to every question, it is important that you get credit for the ones that you do know. Don't miss any questions through careless mistakes. If at all possible, try to take a second to look back over your answer selection and make sure you've selected the correct answer choice and haven't made a costly careless mistake (such as marking an answer choice that you didn't mean to mark). This quick double check should more than pay for itself in caught mistakes for the time it costs.

⊘ Pace Yourself

It's easy to be overwhelmed when you're looking at a page full of questions; your mind is confused and full of random thoughts, and the clock is ticking down faster than you would like. Calm down and maintain the pace that you have set for yourself. Especially as you get down to the last few minutes of the test, don't let the small numbers on the clock make you panic. As long as you are on track by monitoring your pace, you are guaranteed to have time for each question.

⊘ Don't Rush

It is very easy to make errors when you are in a hurry. Maintaining a fast pace in answering questions is pointless if it makes you miss questions that you would have gotten right otherwise. Test writers like to include distracting information and wrong answers that seem right. Taking a little extra time to avoid careless mistakes can make all the difference in your test score. Find a pace that allows you to be confident in the answers that you select.

⊘ Keep Moving

Panicking will not help you pass the test, so do your best to stay calm and keep moving. Taking deep breaths and going through the answer elimination steps you practiced can help to break through a stress barrier and keep your pace.

Final Notes

The combination of a solid foundation of content knowledge and the confidence that comes from practicing your plan for applying that knowledge is the key to maximizing your performance on test day. As your foundation of content knowledge is built up and strengthened, you'll find that the strategies included in this chapter become more and more effective in helping you quickly sift through the distractions and traps of the test to isolate the correct answer.

Now that you're preparing to move forward into the test content chapters of this book, be sure to keep your goal in mind. As you read, think about how you will be able to apply this information on the test. If you've already seen sample questions for the test and you have an idea of the question format and style, try to come up with questions of your own that you can answer based on what you're reading. This will give you valuable practice applying your knowledge in the same ways you can expect to on test day.

Good luck and good studying!

Reading

Using Print and Digital Resources

Dictionary

A print or digital **dictionary** can be used to find out many things about a word. A dictionary will show the correct pronunciation of a word, provide its meaning, and identify what part of speech the word is. It will also tell how the word was derived—that is, what words it came from originally. A dictionary will have a guide that shows how to sound out the words; it will use symbols to indicate sounds, and will also use sample sounds (the "a" in "bad," for instance). A dictionary lists all of the meanings of a word and the parts of speech the word can be used as.

example \ ig-'zam-pəl\ noun
1. something that shows what a group of things is like
2. a model that should be either copied or avoided
3. a punishment meant to serve as a warning to others

Example:

Julia used her dictionary to check the various meanings of the word *clear*. She found this entry:

clear (klîr) adjective
1. obvious.
2. easily seen through
3. free from flaw or blemish
4. free from guilt; untroubled
5. out of the way
6. to tidy *v*
7. to free *v*
8. to earn *v*

Identify which definition of *clear* is used in the following sentence:

Janet stood *clear* of the crowd pushing to get through the door.

The correct answer is meaning 5: "out of the way." If you substitute that definition for the word, the sentence makes sense. Meanings 1, 2, 3, and 4 do not fit with the context of the sentence. Meanings 6, 7, and 8 are verbs and "clear" as it is used in the sample is an adjective. When considering which meaning is being used, always check for context clues in the sentence or in the sentences before or after the sentence in which the word is used. Dictionaries also tell you how to pronounce words and often the derivation of the word, although that is not given here.

Thesaurus

A **thesaurus** is a reference book that gives synonyms of words. It is different from a dictionary because a thesaurus does not give definitions. A thesaurus can be helpful in finding the meaning of an unfamiliar word when reading. If the meaning of a synonym is known, then the meaning of the unfamiliar word will be known. Another time in which a thesaurus can be helpful is when writing. Using a thesaurus helps authors to vary their word choice.

Glossary

A **glossary** is a list of terms and their definitions that can be found at the back of certain types of books, such as textbooks or reference books. A glossary does not have the definitions of all words, like a dictionary, but instead gives the definitions of the important terms within that particular book which are either uncommon or newly introduced. One may use a glossary when reading a book about economics or a chapter in a science textbook, for example, to define some of the technical terms within the text.

Denotative and Connotative Meanings

The **denotative meaning** of a word is the exact dictionary definition of the word. The **connotative meaning** of a word is the emotion conveyed by the use of the word in context. The word may have associated meaning in addition to its dictionary definition. For example, the word *home* is defined in the dictionary as a place where a person or people live. When a reader sees the word in the following context: "Marisol walked briskly *home*, where the smell of fresh-baked apple pie wafted through the warm kitchen," the reader will associate the meaning of the word with coziness and a feeling of well-being. The connotative meaning of a word in a passage can be found by looking at the context clues.

Example

Determine the connotative meaning of the word *ancient* in the following sentence.

> Amy pulled an *ancient* calculator out of the desk, and sat down to figure out how to use it.

In the example, the word 'ancient' literally means very old. The connotative meaning of the word ancient suggests that the calculator does not work as well as more modern versions. in technology, ancient is relative to what is currently being used. For example, a computer may be out of date in a couple years, whereas an ancient society may date back several thousand years.

Use Context to Clarify the Meaning of Words

Finding Word Meanings

Readers of all levels will encounter words that they have either never seen or that they have seen before but still don't know what it means. The best way to define a word in **context** is to look for nearby words that can assist in learning the meaning of the word.

Context Clues

Context clues are hints about the meaning of a word. They are the words or phrases in the sentence or sentences before and after a new or unfamiliar word. **Context clues** give the reader an idea about what a word means. A context clue may also contain words that help define the new word or an example of what the new word means. A context clue in the form of an example may contain the words including 'such as', a dash, or a colon before stated information.

Using context clues to figure out meaning can be helpful when learning a new set of vocabulary words or reading a difficult text. The dictionary definition of a word can always be looked up to double-check intended meaning.

Review Video: Reading Comprehension: Using Context Clues
Visit mometrix.com/academy and enter code: 613660

SYNONYMS AND ANTONYMS

When you understand how words relate to each other, you will discover more in a passage. This is explained by understanding **synonyms** (words that mean the same thing) and **antonyms** (words that mean the opposite of one another). As an example, *dry* and *arid* are synonyms, and *dry* and *wet* are antonyms.

EXAMPLE 1

Read the following sentence from the *Secret Garden* by Frances Hodgson Burnett and determine the meaning of the word *pattering* based on context clues.

> "I like you! I like you!" she cried out, *pattering* down the walk; and she chirped and tried to whistle, which last she did not know how to do in the least.

In the example sentence, the words 'down the walk' show that the character is moving on a sidewalk. The reader knows that the character is crying out and trying to chirp and whistle while moving, so the character cannot be completely out of breath. The character is also trying to reach the person or thing that she is crying out to. from these context clues, the reader can guess that the word *pattering* means to walk quickly.

EXAMPLE 2

Using context clues, determine the meaning of the word *pestilent* in the following excerpt from *Rip Van Winkle* by Washington Irving

> In fact, he declared it was of no use to work on his farm; it was the most *pestilent* little piece of ground in the whole country; everything about it went wrong, and would go wrong in spite of him.

In the example, the word *pestilent* is used to describe the ground. The character states that it was of no use to work on his farm and that everything about it went wrong. This indicates that the ground was difficult to work with, since the character had trouble with the ground no matter what he tried ('and would go wrong in spite of him'). The reader can assume, from these observations, that the word *pestilent* means troublesome, annoying, or not allowing anything to grow, since this example is about the ground on a farm.

EXAMPLE 3

Read the following sentences and determine the meaning of the word *reluctant* based on context clues:

> Sam was *reluctant* to be in the play, so he told the director that he was too busy to rehearse and didn't go to tryouts. He felt too shy to get up on a stage.

In this example sentence, the words "too busy" show that Sam made an excuse about why he couldn't be in the school play. The sentence also says that he "didn't go to tryouts." the second example sentence has other clues. It says, "He felt too shy to get up on stage." These clues give the reader hints about what the word *reluctant* means. It means "not willing."

Substitution to Find Meaning

One way to find out if you have figured out the correct meaning of a new word is to substitute the meaning for the word. Using the example for *reluctant*, if the reader substituted in "not willing," the sentence would read

> Sam was "not willing" to be in the play, so he told the director that he was too busy to rehearse and didn't go to tryouts. He felt to shy to get up on a stage.

This is a way for the reader to confirm that they have used the context clues in the sentence correctly.

Synonyms and Antonyms

When you understand how words relate to each other, you will discover more in a passage. This is explained by understanding **synonyms** (words that mean the same thing) and **antonyms** (words that mean the opposite of one another). As an example, *dry* and *arid* are synonyms, and *dry* and *wet* are antonyms.

Multiple-Meaning Words

A multiple-meaning word has different definitions, depending on the contextual use of the word. A multiple-meaning word is also called a **homonym**. A homonym is defined as a word that has more than one meaning, but is spelled and pronounced the same for all of them. For example, look at the word *leaves* in the following two sentences:

1. Michelle *leaves* the building at 5 o'clock every day.
2. The *leaves* fell off the oak tree in September.

In the first sentence, *leaves* means exits. in the second sentence, *leaves* refers to parts of a tree. By looking at the rest of each sentence, the reader can understand which definition of the multiple-meaning word the author is referring to.

Similar Words

Homophones are words that are pronounced the same, but may be spelled differently. an example of two homophones would be *heir* (someone due to inherit an estate) and *air* (the invisible substance people breathe).

Homographs are words that are spelled the same, but may be pronounced differently. an example of a homograph is the word *row*, which is pronounced one way when used to mean a horizontal grouping and is pronounced another way when used to mean an argument.

Using Roots to Determine Meaning

Affixes and Roots

A **root word** is a word that can be added onto. an **affix** is a prefix or suffix that is added onto a root word. Often, the affixes in the English language come from Latin or Greek origins. A **prefix** is added to the beginning of a root word and a **suffix** is added to the end of a root word. When you look at the meaning of a root word and the meaning of any affixes added to the root word, you can figure out the approximate meaning of the word. For example, the root word "happy" means "to be content." the prefix "un-" means "not." the reader can therefore figure out that "unhappy" means to "not being content."

COMMON PREFIXES

Prefix	Meaning	Example
dis-	not	disagree (not agree)
im-	not	impossibly (not possible)
in-	in, into, not	injustice (not just)
mis-	wrongly	misspell (to spell wrongly)
non-	not	nonpaid (not paid)
pre-	before	preview (to view before)
sub-	under	submerge (to sink below the surface)
super-	over or greater than	superhuman (greater than a regular human
trans-	across, through, or change	translate (to write or say in a different language)

COMMON GREEK ROOT-WORDS

Root	Meaning	Example
auto	self	automobile (a self-propelled vehicle)
geo	earth or ground	geography (study of the earth)
graph	writing	graphic (art, especially involving drawing or lettering)
meter	measure	thermometer (an instrument for measuring temperature)
photo	light	photon (a small particle of light)

Common Suffixes

Suffix	Meaning	Example
-able	can be done	likeable (can be liked)
-er	a person connected with	teacher (a person connected with teaching)
-it/ity	state of	activity (state of being active)
-ful	full of	wonderful (full of wonder)
-ive	cause to, tend to, or doing	creative (a person who tends to make new things or think of new ideas)
-ness	state of being	darkness (being dark)
-ology	study of	biology (study of life)
-y	characterized by	cloudy (characterized by clouds)

Example 1

Determine the meaning of the word "misconception" based on its root and affixes.

The word "misconception" is made up of three sections: a root, a prefix, and a suffix. to figure out the meaning of the word, you need to analyze these parts of the word individually. The root *concept* means "idea." It comes from the Latin word *conceptus* meaning "something conceived. There are two affixes in the word. The prefix *mis-* means "not" or "bad." the suffix *-tion* means "action" or "process." Put these meanings together and the word "misconception" means "the act of having a bad idea" or "misunderstanding."

Studying roots and affixes is important because it allows you to decode words that you might not otherwise understand with relative ease.

Main Idea and Supporting Details

Main Idea and Supporting Details

The main idea in a passage is usually located in the first paragraph or two of text. Having the main idea near the beginning of the passage allows the author to grab the reader's attention and let them know what the rest of the passage will discuss.

To find the main idea in a passage, there are questions the reader can ask while reading: What is this passage about? What does the author want the reader to know about the topic? the supporting details will provide evidence that the main idea is correct and are found in the body of a passage. The supporting details often provide examples of the main idea.

For example, a passage may contain the main idea: "Ellis Island was an entry-point to America for many immigrants during the Industrial Revolution." a supporting detail for the main idea may be "Immigrants were examined for contagious diseases at Ellis Island before being granted entry to America."

Review Video: Thesis Statements
Visit mometrix.com/academy and enter code: 691033

EXAMPLE 1

Determine the main idea the following sentence tells the reader and indicate what details support the main idea:

> Her breath billowed out in clouds of white and disappeared into the quiet air.

The main idea is what the author wants the reader to understand about the text. Details help to explain or support that main idea. A main idea usually states the point of an entire essay, article, or book, but can be simply stated in one sentence. The main idea in the sentence above is that a girl is outside in the cold. Details to support this statement include the word 'her,' showing that the character is a girl, and 'clouds of white,' which indicate that the air is cold. in order to conclude that the girl is out in the cold, the reader needs to understand that breath can be seen when the air is cold.

SUPPORTING DETAILS

Provide evidence and backing for the main point. All texts contain details, but they are only classified as supporting details when they serve to reinforce some larger point. Supporting details are most commonly found in informative and persuasive texts. in some cases, they will be clearly indicated with words like **for example** or **for instance**, or they will begin with words like **first**, **second**, and **last**. However, these special words are not a requirement. As a reader, it is important to consider whether the author's supporting details really back up his or her main point. Supporting details can be factual and correct but still not relevant to the author's point. Sometimes, supporting details can seem important but they might not support the main idea in the story well because they are based on opinion that cannot be proven.

EXAMPLE 2

Decide whether the following sentence is the main point or a supporting point of a text, and state where the information would be placed in an outline:

> One type of horseback riding, bareback horseback riding, involves sitting on a moving horse without a saddle and grasping the horse's mane.

This sentence is a supporting point, with the main point of the entire text likely about horseback riding in general. As a supporting point, this sentence would go further down in an outline, next to any numeral after numeral I. This sentence can be followed by additional sub-points that further explain the concept of bareback horseback riding. When a supporting point is used to clarify a main point or topic, the supporting point helps to break the topic down into smaller pieces.

Opposite Point of View

After identifying the main idea, readers can increase their understanding of the text if they think about what the opposite point of view would be.

Read the following topic sentence. Describe what the opposite point of view would include:

> The new bike path at the public park provides families in the community with a safe opportunity to get some fresh air on the weekends.

This topic sentence could be taken in several different directions. The main focus of the sentence is that the bike path is safe and allows for families to get out and enjoy some fresh air on the weekends. The opposite point of view may state that the new bike path is unsafe and the air is polluted. an example of a topic sentence with the opposite point of view may state: the new bike path at Primer School is unsafe for families in the community to travel on the weekends and goes through a polluted area.

When looking for the main point in a sentence, look for keywords that define the sentence. in the sentence about the bike path, we know that the path is new, seems safe, and has fresh air. By changing around these keywords, the entire meaning of the sentence can be shifted.

Themes

The Theme of a Story

The **theme** of a story is the lesson that it teaches, or the message the author wants to get across. The theme is linked to the characters, the setting, and the events in a story. A passage can have two or more themes that convey its overall idea.

The theme of a story is not the same as the topic of a story. The topic is what the story is about, but the theme is what a reader is meant to learn. When readers are discussing theme, they can determine both theme topics as well as theme statements.

Theme topics are broad ideas that apply to the text. Examples are:

- Love
- The importance of friendship
- Good vs. evil
- The circle of life

Theme statements are specific ideas that must be written in sentence form, and usually contain the name of the work and the author. Examples are:

- In *The City of Ember* by Jeanne DuPrau, the author shows how acts of courage can bring positive changes to the world.
- The author of *The Indian in the Cupboard*, Lynne Reid Banks, introduces readers to a world of imagination where the meaning of true friendship is explored.

Some themes are fairly common. These themes are called **universal themes** and they suggest things about life, society, and human nature.

Themes are very rarely stated in the text. Instead, the reader has to **infer** the theme by reading closely and thinking carefully about what the author is saying.

Themes are an important part of literature because they serve the purpose of teaching the reader or listener a truth about life. The theme is developed by how a character or characters respond to their situations and challenges.

Example 1

Explain why "Take care of what you care about" accurately describes the theme of the following excerpt.

> Luca collected baseball cards. But Luca wasn't very careful with them. He left them around the house. His dog liked to chew. Luca and his friend Bart were looking at his collection. Then, they went outside. When Luca got home, he saw his dog chewing on his cards. They were ruined.

This excerpt tells the story of a boy who is careless with his baseball cards and leaves them lying around. His dog ends up chewing them and ruining them. The lesson is that if you care about something, you need to take care of it. This is the point of the story. The theme is the lesson that a story teaches. Some stories have more than one theme, but this is not really true of this excerpt. The reader needs to figure out the theme based on what happens in the story. Sometimes, as in the case of fables, the theme is stated directly in the text. However, this is not usually the case.

Example 2

Read the following passage and explain why "It is better not to run away" describes the story's theme.

> Ivan made fun of Sasha. So Sasha was scared of him. If he saw Ivan coming, Sasha hid. Then Sasha changed. He stopped hiding from Ivan. If Ivan laughed at him, Sasha laughed right back. He wasn't afraid anymore. Soon, Ivan stopped making fun of Sasha. This made Sasha feel happier.

The theme "It is better not to run away" fits what happens in the story. Sasha is scared of Ivan and hides from him. But then Sasha stops hiding and laughs back at Ivan, and after that he is not afraid anymore. For him it was better not to run away, but to stay and face his fears. in the end Sasha is happier. He solved his problem. This is the theme that the story teaches through the events of the story. Sasha and the reader learn that something good happened when Sasha did not hide or run away. This is the message of this passage. The reader needs to figure out the theme from what happens in a story.

Paraphrasing and Summarizing

Paraphrasing and Summarizing

Paraphrasing and summarizing are two ways readers can work to understand what they read. Both involve reading a text and recalling the main points in an accurate way, but they differ in several ways.

How to Paraphrase	How to Summarize
State the message in the text in the reader's own words, while keeping the original meaning of the text Take all of the original ideas and word them in a way that the reader can better understand Put what the reader has read into their own words, rephrasing what the author has written	State main points of the text clearly and to-the-point. Take information and state it simply, in a much shorter form. Put information in a short form that keeps the main points of the whole text. Do not include many details, just the main idea of the text

Paraphrasing is often done for individual ideas, while summarizing is done for an entire block of text or ideas. Often times, a summary can be done in just one sentence, boiling down the author's words into just main idea.

Review Video: Summarizing Text
Visit mometrix.com/academy and enter code: 172903

Paraphrasing Main Point of a Sentence

Paraphrase the main point of the following two sentences:

> Emmanuel went swimming in the lake by his house, where the water reached a depth of twenty feet in the middle. He did not venture out more than six feet into the water, however.

When paraphrasing a couple sentences or an entire paragraph, always include the main point of the text being reviewed, this is what the reader needs to know about the text. in the example, the reader needs to know that Emmanuel went swimming in the lake, but not more than six feet out. A paraphrase of the text may include: Emmanuel went swimming six feet out in the lake by his house. That is the main point that the audience needs to know.

Recall that a paraphrase is stating the author's ideas in the reader's own words. A summary typically involves including the main points of a longer text, such as a novel or full story.

Summarizing Literature to Support Comprehension

When reading literature, especially demanding works, summarizing helps readers identify important information and organize it in their minds. They can also identify themes, problems, and solutions, and can sequence the story. Readers can summarize before, during, and after they read. They should use their own words, as they do when describing a personal event or giving directions. Previewing a text's organization before reading by examining the book cover, table of contents, and illustrations also aids summarizing. So does making notes of key words and ideas in a graphic organizer while reading. Graphic organizers are another useful method; readers skim the text to determine main ideas and then narrow the list with the aid of the organizer. Unimportant details should be omitted in summaries. Summaries can include description, problem-solution, comparison-contrast, sequence, main ideas, and cause-and-effect.

Evaluation of Summaries

A summary of a literary passage is a **short version** of the passage's main points in the reader's own words. Several guidelines can be used in evaluating a summary. The summary should be complete yet concise. It should be accurate, balanced, fair, neutral, and objective, excluding the reader's own opinions or reactions. It should reflect in similar proportion how much each point summarized was covered in the original passage. Summary writers should include tags of attribution, like "Macaulay argues that" to reference the original author whose ideas are represented in the summary. Summary writers should not overuse quotations: they should only quote central concepts or phrases they cannot precisely convey in words other than those of the original author. Another aspect in evaluating a summary is whether it can stand alone as a coherent, unified composition. in addition, evaluation of a summary should include whether its writer has cited the original source of the passage so that readers can find it.

Example Summary

Read the following paragraph and then give a one sentence summary statement:

> When choosing a pet, people need to think about what type of home they can offer the animal. For example, a small apartment might not be a good fit for a large dog, but could be a comfortable home for a kitten. A house that has a big yard would be great for a puppy, but a rabbit does not need a large yard.

In order to summarize, one has to identify the main idea and any supporting ideas in the author's work. The summary is an overview of the author's paragraph and will tell what it is about without getting into any of the details. The summary needs to be broad enough to cover all of the information in the author's paragraph. Here is a possible summary statement for the above paragraph:

> People need to consider a number of factors, particularly the available space they have, when choosing a pet.

Example Paraphrasing

Read the following sentences and then paraphrase the material:

> Phillipe is debating which elective he should take next year. He is considering choir, band, and soccer. He is making a list of pros and cons to talk about it with his mom so that he is sure to make the right choice.

When paraphrasing information, one needs to read carefully and pay attention to details, then put the material away and write or tell it in their own words. One does not want to look at the material while paraphrasing to avoid plagiarizing by accident. Here is one example of a way to paraphrase the sentences:

> Phillipe has to choose a new elective for his schedule. His choices are choir, band, and soccer. He wants to make the right choice, so he's making a list of pros and cons and planning to talk to his mom.

Objective Summary

An **objective summary** of an informational text tells what the main idea of the text is and includes the important details. It tells what the text is mostly about and includes the most important supporting details. A summary should not include too much information; it is not a paraphrase of the information. It is important to select only the most important details to include. A summary should also be objective. This is achieved by focusing on the main idea rather than any opinions that might be in the text but that are not related to the main idea. It would also not include any personal opinions on the subject.

Example 1

Read the following summary and explain how to improve it.

> Edgar Degas was a great artist who broke with tradition and became an Impressionist. His paintings and sculptures are included in the collections of major museums everywhere. in his forties, his vision became poor and he worked more on sculptures because he could feel them. He died in 1917 at the age of 83. His father was a banker.

This summary is quite good. It has a main idea and includes some of the important details. The main idea is that Degas was a great artist. Supporting details include that his paintings and sculpture are included in collections of major museums as well as the fact that he had poor vision and turned to sculpting because he could feel the sculptures. While the information about his death is not perhaps the most important, it is of interest that he lived to the age of 83. The one glaring error with the summary is that it mentions the fact that his father was a banker. This does not directly relate to the main idea. It is not a supporting detail and is unimportant to the central thesis of the passage. It should be deleted.

Example 2

Read the following summary and discuss how it could be improved.

> This story is about a man and a woman who moved to the West many years ago. There was a lot of information about covered wagons or "prairie schooners," as they called them. I liked the story because of that.

The summary tells the main idea of the story, but it doesn't include the details of what happens in the story. It does not include the main characters and what they did or what challenges they faced. It does not summarize the plot. Another problem with the summary is that it is not objective; it is subjective. The writer describes what he thinks about the story. But personal opinions have no place in an objective summary of a story. to improve it, the writer should remove his personal opinion and add descriptions of who was in the story, what important things happened to them, and how the story ended.

Plot Elements

Plot

The storyline of any text is also called a **plot**. The characters and events in the story determine what the plot will be. Readers may find a **plot line** useful as they try to put the events in the text in order and determine the relationships between events.

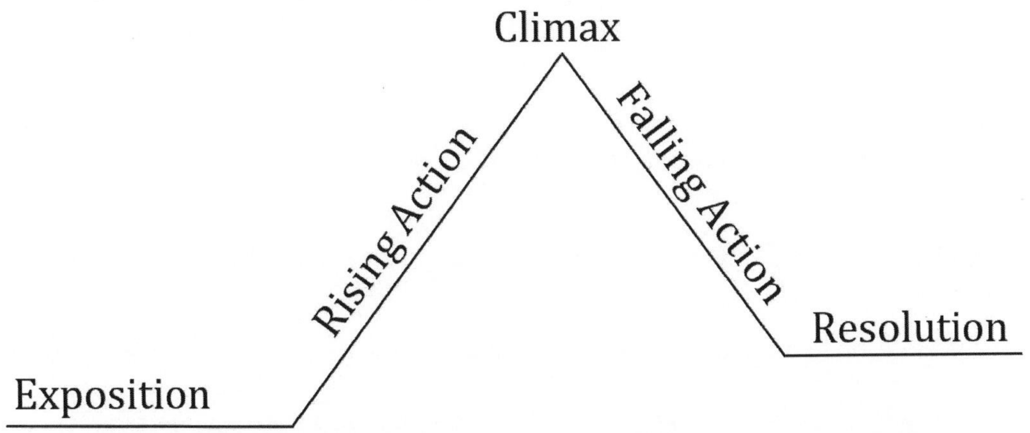

Review Video: Plot Line
Visit mometrix.com/academy and enter code: 944011

Every plot will begin with **exposition**, which introduces the characters and the setting of the story. The plot will continue to develop as new ideas and events centered on the main conflict in the story are revealed, which is called the **rising action**. The action in the story will rise until a **climax** is reached within the conflict. The climax can also be referred to as the turning point in the story, since the climax is where each character makes an important decision. After the climax, the action starts to wind down during the **falling action**. At this point, the characters begin to follow the paths they chose in during climax. The events of the story reach **resolution** in some way by the end of the story. Some conflicts are left open-ended, so that the reader is left to decide what really happened at the end of the story. Keep in mind that not all resolutions are happy or peaceful.

Example

Read the following plot and analyze what event is missing from the plot sequence.

> Martin's family decided to go camping at the local park over the weekend. They packed all the camping necessities and drove to the park. Thick sheets of rain poured down all day, so they were stuck in their tent.

Martin and his family forgot to check the weather forecast before they left for their camping trip. to fill in the missing detail, the author may write: "Martin and his family checked the forecast and saw that it was going to rain, but decided to go camping anyway." the flow of the story is broken up by the sudden realization that it is raining, something that could be prevented by adding in the missing detail.

When details are missing from a plot sequence, the audience has trouble following the action in a story. By adding in additional details, the point of each step in a story can be made clearer to the audience.

Identifying the Main Conflict

An important part of analyzing the plot of a passage is identifying the **main conflict**. There will likely be many smaller conflicts in the story, but there will be one main problem that influences the characters and events. to identify the main conflict, first look at who the main character is. Now ask yourself what they want. They may want to something to happen or not happen, another character to do or not do something, or to confront or avoid a problem, among other things. Once you know what they want, now ask yourself what is standing in the character's way. It may be a person, an event, or something less tangible like the passing of time. Combining what the main character wants and why they do not currently have leaves the reader with a summary of the main conflict.

Example 1

Read the following sentence from the *Call of the Wild* by Jack London and describe the main conflict in the sentence. Explain how the conflict may be resolved.

> The breaking down of discipline likewise affected the dogs in their relations with one another.

Based on the information in the sentence, an event has caused the dogs, the characters in the story, to not follow their regular routine. The sentence indicates that there has been a breaking down of discipline which is affecting how the dogs relate to each other. in order to solve this conflict, discipline needs to be restored. However, in order to return to previous relations between the dogs, any problems that are in the way of conflict resolution need to be taken care of. The word *likewise* means *also*, which tells the reader that other parts of the story are being affected besides the relations between the dogs.

Example 2

Read the following sentence and explain the main conflict between the two characters:

> Joe stared angrily at Jamie's retreating back as Jamie raced away down the field with Joe's soccer ball.

The main conflict in the sentence is that Jamie has Joe's soccer ball. There may be additional conflicts between the two characters, but none are evident from the evidence shown in the sentence. in any story, a conflict may be minor and only affect part of the story, or be the main focus, taking an entire story to solve a conflict between characters. in the context of the sentence, it is not clear whether or not the entire story will revolve around Jamie taking Joe's soccer ball.

Resolution

The term **resolution** usually indicates the result of a conflict in a story. Conflict between characters, within a character, or against an external element is necessary in order to have a plot for a story. without conflict, no events would occur to form the story. A conflict will come to a climax, and then conclude in some way. The resolution of a problem may be open-ended, end tragically, or end in a way that is good for everyone involved. The problem resolution typically occurs near the end of a story, after the climax has happened. A problem may be resolved by the characters involved within the conflict or by an external event; an upcoming resolution may be foreshadowed in the text, or may be completely unexpected by the reader. If the resolution is completely unexpected, it is considered to be a **twist** in the story.

EFFECT OF PLOT ON THEME

The plot builds one event at a time and over time, the plot of the story helps the reader understand the **theme**. The theme of a story is its underlying message, and should not be confused with the story's topic. For example, in a story about a man who goes to war to fight for his country, the topic is war. The theme would be what the author is saying about going to war, perhaps that patriotism should be encouraged in a nation. Themes are most often expressed as a complete sentence in what is called a **theme statement**. an example of a theme statement is "War is a necessary evil and the able-bodied citizens of a nation should fight to defend their freedoms." Themes are always based on the opinions and beliefs of the writer, so an author who does not support war might write a story that could be described by a very different theme statement, such as "War is never an acceptable choice, and citizens should peacefully protest the use of violence to solve problems."

EXAMPLE

Discuss how the following sentence would impact the theme of the passage it belongs to:

> Wanda realized then that she had made a terrible mistake and she would be haunted by this experience for the rest of her life.

This sentence would impact the theme because it suggests that Wanda would never recover from something that she did and that she would remember it for the rest of her life. This ties into a theme because it is saying something about life and what Wanda realizes about her life. We do not know what she did, but the sentence clearly states that it was a mistake. We would have to read the entire passage to understand why it was a mistake and why she would be haunted, but the sentence gives us a good idea that she learned a lesson from what happened.

EFFECT OF PLOT ON A STORY'S CHARACTERS

The plot of a story unfolds as each event follows another, shaping the characters as they react to the various events that occur. Some characters are able to resolve their problems by the end of the story, while some characters fail to overcome their predicaments. As characters respond to the events around them, they reveal more and more about their personalities. Some grow and some do not. The reader can use the events of the plot to interpret the meaning of the story and understand its characters.

EXAMPLE

Read the excerpt and explain how finding the chest affects Marta.

> The map said this was the spot. Marta held her breath. Her fists were clenched into two tight balls. She lifted the shovel and scooped more sand out of the hole. There it was; she had found the chest with the diamonds. She opened the top. She would never need to work again. She smiled. It was really happening.

The event affects Marta by making her happy. The reader gets several clues that she is anxiously waiting ("Marta held her breath" and "her fists were clenched"), and that she is happy with what she found ("She smiled"). Events can cause characters to have all kinds of feelings. Here, something wonderful happened. However, events in stories are not always quite so happy. For instance, if a robber had suddenly seen Marta and the chest, he might have stolen the chest. That event would have had a very different effect on her. Readers need to pay attention to how characters are reacting to events, whether they are simply hinted at or stated in the story. in this way a reader will learn what characters are like.

Setting in Story

Setting

The setting is the time and place in which a story takes place. The setting of a story may stay the same for the entire story or change as events in the story unfold. For example, an entire story may take place in one room or cross continents as the reader follows the characters along on a trail of events.

The setting of a story is described by the author in terms of what it looks like, how the character feels, and anything else that is happening at that location at the time. For example, a character may be caught on a doorstep on a cold, rainy day. The character may feel frustrated as they shiver in the doorway, waiting for the heavy rain to let up a bit.

Shaping a Character with Setting or Plot

The setting of a story shapes character because it helps to define the situation that a character finds herself in. A character is limited to the setting of a story. For example, if a story takes place in a cold environment filled with snow and ice, this is certain to impact what actions a character can and will take. Frequently, the setting changes the way characters behave based on time. For example, the character of a woman who is a single mother in 1920 would be seen and behave very differently than a single mother in 2020.

Example

Read the excerpt and determine how the setting influences the character in this excerpt.

> She had swum too far out. The waves were higher than she thought. She was struggling hard to get to shore. She wondered if she would make it. She thought of her childhood. Had she been right to run away from home, she wondered? Just then, a lifeguard grabbed her and helped her to shore.

The setting of the ocean and the high waves creates a conflict in the character. She is worried. She thinks about her childhood and her parents. She doesn't know if she will make it to shore. This is how the setting affects the character in this excerpt. without the high waves and the struggle, she would not become so worried and start to think about her past. She probably would not have questioned herself. This is an example of how a setting influences a character. If the waves had not been high, there probably would not have been a struggle or any self-searching of the swimmer's past.

Perception of a Story Based on Setting

The setting of a story can allow the reader to draw on personal experience about where the story takes place. If a story takes place on a farm, the reader will likely picture a rural, peaceful setting, which may go along with (or be in contrast to) the actual plot of the story. For example, a reader would not expect a scary story to occur on a farm on a sunny day. Conversely, a reader may view a dark subway as a dangerous place, while the plot of a story set there may be based on a very calm series of events. When an author is crafting a story, they need to consider what the audience may already think about a particular setting in order to properly present the events of a story for greatest impact.

Historical and Cultural Setting

Historical context influences literature in a number of ways. The style of the author's writing can be impacted by the historical period during which it was written (e.g., Dickens wrote at a time when authors were paid by the word; this is why his novels are so long). Obviously, the setting of the book includes its historical context. in addition, dialect may be a function of the historical period of the book. When a reader understands the historical context of a particular book, he or she can have a deeper understanding of the novel. Knowing about the time period during which the author wrote, as well as the time period discussed in the novel, helps the reader understand some of the author's choices, including character motivations.

Literary Devices

Points of View

The point of view of a text is the perspective from which it is told. Every literary text has a narrator or person who tells the story. The two main points of view that authors most often use are first person and third person.

First person

- Tells a story through the eyes of one character.
- Uses the pronouns 'I,' 'me,' 'we,' and 'my.'
- The reader gets only one side of the story, without any other angles on what may have happened in the text

Third person

- Tells a story about a character or group of characters from an outside viewpoint.
- Uses the words 'her', 'his,' 'they,' or a name to talk about a character or characters.
- A common way to show action in a story which allows the author to easily and realistically tell a story from more than one person's viewpoint.
- Gives readers a more complete view of a story as it is told from many different perspectives.

Second person

- Second person is an uncommon point of view in literature that uses the pronoun 'you.' Second person is usually reserved for speaking directly to someone, often when giving instructions.
- Examples might include: "Go get me a fork" or "will you wash the dishes?"

Review Video: Point of View
Visit mometrix.com/academy and enter code: 383336

Different Forms of Third Person

When an author writes in third-person point of view, there are a few options to choose from:

- **Third person omniscient** - There is an all-knowing narrator telling the story as well as interpreting events, and relating thoughts of the characters.
- **Third person limited (or closed)** - The author writes in the third person, but does so from only one character's point of view. There are two different variations of this type of narration: the narrator can either stay with the same character throughout or cycle through different characters over the course of the story.

Connecting to a Text

Making Connections to Enhance Comprehension

Reading involves thinking. For good comprehension, readers make text-to-self, text-to-text, and text-to-world connections. Making connections helps readers understand text better and predict what might occur next based on what they already know, such as how characters in the story feel or what happened in another text. Readers can make connections before, during, and after reading. Venn diagrams and other graphic organizers can help readers visualize connections.

Text-to-Self

Reading while looking for connections with the reader's life and experiences makes literature more personally relevant and meaningful to readers. Sentences showing text-to-self connections may begin with these examples:

- This reminds me of a time when...
- I understand how the character feels because...
- The setting makes me think of...
- I experienced this same thing when...

Text-to-Text

Reading while looking for connections to other texts helps the reader learn to identify the way authors use genre, setting, characters, plot elements, literary structure and devices, and themes to create meaning. Sentences showing text-to-text connections may begin with these examples:

- The character in this story reminds me of the character in...
- These two stories are alike because...
- The conflict in this story is similar to the conflict in...
- The relationship between the friends in this story is different than the relationship in...

Text-to-World

Reading while looking for connections to the world helps the reader begin to see literature as a reflection of real life and notice patterns in history and current events. Sentences showing text-to-world connections may begin with these examples:

- The event in this story sounds like the event in history when...
- The actions of this character sound like...
- This is like what happened in real life when...
- I heard about this on the news when...

Making Inferences

Inference

An **inference** is a **conclusion** or generalization that the reader makes based on the information provided within a text. Certain facts are included to help a reader come to a specific conclusion. It is what the story may hint about, and what a reader can conclude as a result of what the author says in the passage. It is also the best guess that a reader can make based on what happened or was said or in a story. A good inference is based on or supported by details in the passage.

Readers may come to their own conclusion about a topic, or the author may state a conclusion at the end of a story. When readers are in the middle of a story, they can predict what will happen at the end of it based on the events that have occurred so far and the typical characteristics that have been presented by the author up to that point. A reader needs to consider all of the information that an author has presented, including the main point and supporting points, to make logical conclusions and inferences about the story.

For instance, if a passage says that Joan is holding her mouth and moaning, you might conclude, or **infer,** that she has a sore mouth or a toothache. You cannot be sure of this, but it is the best conclusion that you can reach using the information at hand. Inferences are considered **implicit information**. They are not found directly in a passage.

Review Video: Inference
Visit mometrix.com/academy and enter code: 379203

Finding Explicit Information

Explicit information is the term for information that is directly stated in a story or passage. It is what the author tells you. It is not information that is hinted at or that you have to make a conclusion about. Explicit information can be facts or details about an event, something or someone. There is usually a lot of explicit information in a story and this information is often used to make an inference or draw a conclusion. to answer questions that ask about explicit information, simply reread the story until you find the answer. in fiction, details about characters, events, and setting are often explicit.

Example 1

Read the following excerpt and tell what information is explicit.

> From his bed, Steve could see the moon begin to rise and the stars twinkle. He could hear the nurses as they walked down the long hall, their footsteps echoing in the quiet.

The explicit information in the excerpt is all about Steve and what he could see and hear. The passage says that he could see the moon begin to rise and the stars twinkle from his bed. It also says that he could hear the nurses walking down the hall. This is explicit information. The author is describing what Steve can see and hear. There is nothing that is hinted at in the excerpt except that Steve seems to be in a hospital. However, that conclusion is not explicit information. The author does not say this directly, so it is implicit information.

Example 2

Read the following excerpt and tell what you can conclude about why Vicki got a cold.

> Hi Nance,
>
> Richard and I went camping last weekend. A bear ate all our food while we were sleeping. and it was cold and rainy the last night. We have both caught colds. Next time we go camping we are going to bring warmer clothes and extra food for the bears.
>
> Love, Vicki

You can conclude that Vicki got a cold because it was cold and rainy on the last night of her camping trip. She also talks about bringing warmer clothes the next time she goes camping, which further suggests that she was cold. However, the fact that a bear ate her food would have little to do with her getting sick, so that is not the reason she got a cold. It is logical to conclude that she got a cold because of the weather and not having warmer clothes. It is the best inference that you can make from the letter. Inferences are the best guesses that a reader can make based on the information in a passage.

Example 3

Read the following sentence. Draw a conclusion based upon the information presented:

> The hilltop was covered in low-lying clouds of grey, and a moist silence hung in the air as if the sky had drawn in a breath and paused.

The reader can conclude, or infer, based on the information in the sentence, that it is about to rain on the hilltop. The words used in the sentence give the reader clues to draw this conclusion. For example, the words low-lying clouds of grey indicate that rainclouds are present. A moist silence often occurs just before a storm. Based on the reader's own experience and the words presented in the sentence, the reader can conclude that the storm is about to break. Authors will often only present a certain amount of detail to the reader, and the reader needs to fill in the blanks. an author will give the reader just enough information to come to a logical conclusion without having to directly state that conclusion in the story.

Using Evidence to Support a Response

Text Evidence

The term **text evidence** refers to information included in a text that supports the main point of the paper. A reader can draw conclusions or generalizations based upon information found in a text, in which the author will deliberately include key points that serve as supporting details for the main point. For example, the main point of a paper may state: the average yearly rainfall in the city has risen by 2 inches per year in the past five years. The paper would go on to include the amount of rainfall for each month or season and any contributing factors that may be causing an increase in yearly rainfall. Additional facts, or text evidence to support the point that yearly rainfall is rising in the city would help to prove that the author's main point is correct. in fiction, details about characters, events, and setting can be both explicit and implicit.

Review Video: Textual Evidence
Visit mometrix.com/academy and enter code: 486236

Explicit Information

Explicit information includes facts and statements that are found directly in a passage or a story. It is not information that is hinted at or information you need to make a conclusion about. Explicit information may be found in many forms; it can be contained in a quote as well as in a description. It can be found in dialogue and in actions. This information can sometimes be used to support an inference. The answers to questions about explicit information are found through careful reading of the text. Attention is given to important facts or other information.

Example:

Read the following excerpt and tell what information is explicit:

> Carlos didn't really speak Spanish. His parents often spoke to him in that language, which he understood, but he always replied in English. As a result, his Spanish pronunciation was very bad, and he had trouble picking the right word. But then he fell in love with Alicia, who didn't understand English. Carlos changed very quickly.

The explicit information in the excerpt is all about Carlos. The passage says that he didn't really speak Spanish. It says that while his parents spoke to him in Spanish and that he understood it, he always responded in English. It also says his Spanish pronunciation was bad and he didn't pick the right words. This is explicit information. So is the fact that Carlos fell in love with Alicia and that Carlos changed quickly.

Implicit Information

Implicit information is information that is not directly stated in a text, but can be inferred from something that the author explicitly states. For instance, the author may say "Seth buys a new TV, laptop, and home theater system every year." from this the reader could infer several things. For instance, Seth probably likes electronics and has a lot of spending money.

Example

Draw a conclusion based on the implicit information in the following sentence from the *Adventures of Tom Sawyer* by Mark Twain:

> He had discovered a great law of human action, without knowing it—namely, that in order to make a man or a boy covet a thing, it is only necessary to make the thing difficult to attain.

The reader can clearly see from the sentence that the character did not set out to learn something, but through an action, the character learned that people will want what is hard to attain. Although it's not explicitly stated, the reader can draw the conclusion that the character gained the experience of coveting (or desiring) something that was hard to get.

Drawing Conclusions Based On Text Evidence

Readers often need to use prior experience and background information to draw an accurate conclusion about the passage they are reading. Sometimes interpreting the information in a sentence can be difficult, especially if the reader is unfamiliar with some of the words used in a sentence. Looking at the words that the reader does understand in the sentence can help. By taking a pen or pencil and underlining important information in a sentence, the reader can better understand what the author is trying to say and draw a clearer conclusion from that.

Example 1

Draw a conclusion based on the following sentence.

New Orleans then was a mere huddle of buildings around Jackson Square; but with the purchase of the Louisiana territory from France, and the great influx of American enterprise that characterized the first quarter of the last century, development was working like yeast...

The sentence describes how New Orleans grew after the "purchase of the Louisiana territory" and how "development was working like yeast". Yeast multiplies rapidly, so the reader can conclude that New Orleans was growing rapidly.

Example 2

Read the following sentence. Draw a conclusion based upon the information presented.

"A rosy-faced servant-maid opened the door, and smiled as she took the letter which he silently offered."

The reader can conclude, based on the sentence, that the servant-maid is friendly. The words "rosy-faced" and "smiled" lead the reader to this conclusion. People who are friendly are often described as having rosy complexions and smiling as a common sign of pleasantness. The reader can also assume, from the sentence, that the letter does not present any threat or unpleasantness to the servant-maid. The person presenting the letter does not have anything to say upon offering it, so perhaps he is waiting to see how the servant-maid will react.

When interpreting a sentence, always look for key words that describe a character. The author carefully crafts a description of each character, to form a picture in the reader's mind about what the character is like.

Synthesizing Information

Synthesizing a Text with Existing Knowledge

Synthesizing is similar to summarizing but it takes it one step further. Synthesizing involves taking the main points of a text and comparing it with existing knowledge to create a new idea, perspective, or way of thinking.

Another term for knowledge that you already have is **schema**. The plural form of this word is **schemata**. Schemata contain all the ideas you have about something. Synthesizing is all about how schemata change over time with the introduction of new information.

Example

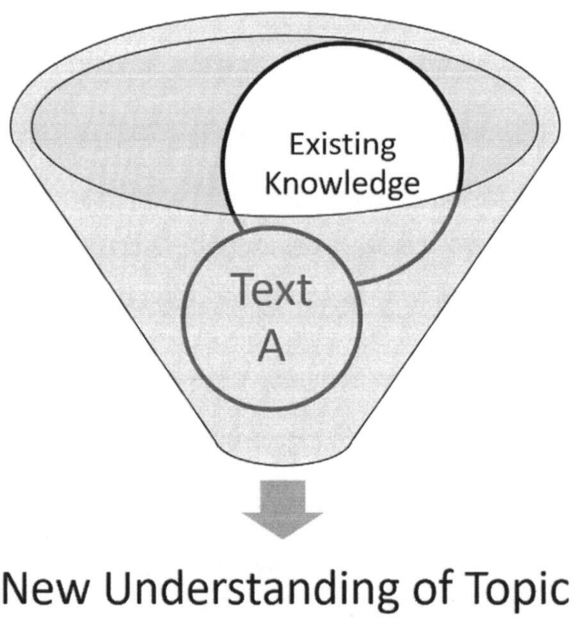

Using self-questioning strategies can help readers synthesize texts with their schemata to increase or change their understanding of topics. These questions include

- What do I already know about this topic?
- Is any of this new information?
- Has my perspective changed now that I've read this?
- What do I understand now that I didn't before?

- What are the main ideas of this text?
- How do the parts of the text fit together to create meaning?
- Are there any text-to-text, text-to-self, or text-to-world connections here?

SYNTHESIZING TEXTS WITHOUT EXISTING KNOWLEDGE

If the reader is completely unfamiliar with the topic, they will have no background knowledge. in this case, instead of using existing knowledge, synthesizing may instead be done by combining the ideas provided in two or three different texts. The reader must make connections between the texts, determine how the ideas fit together, and gather evidence to support the new perspective.

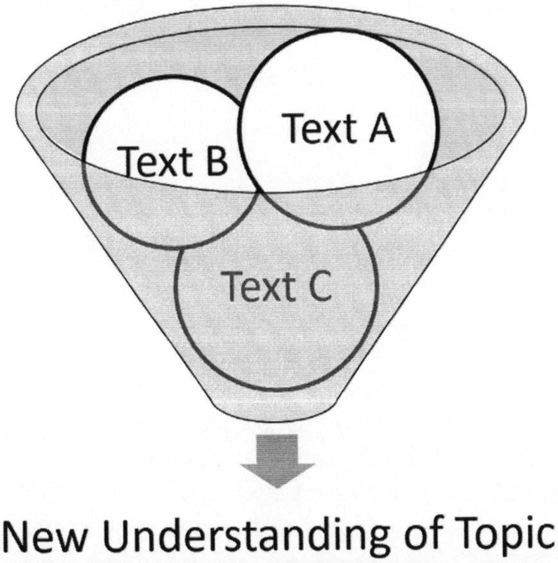

Using self-questioning strategies can help readers synthesize texts to increase their understanding of topics. in this case, readers are creating new schemata as they read. Common questions include:

- What do these texts have in common?
- What is different between these texts?
- What new information have I learned?
- What do I understand now that I didn't before?
- How do these texts relate to one another?
- If I think of these texts as parts of one whole, what meaning do they create together?
- What predictions can I make about this topic?

Literary Genres

LITERARY GENRES

Literature contains many different **genres**, which are categories that texts can be divided into. Genres are used to group types of writing together for purposes of study, reading, or simple organization. Some common literary genres are

- **Realistic fiction** -A story that could actually happen and reflects life in a realistic way.
- **Adventure stories** -Short, mostly fictional stories that follow characters as they go on an adventure or quest.

- **Historical fiction** -Often strays from historical reality in order to tell a story and make a true historical event more interesting to the reader.
- **Mysteries** -Fiction stories about solving crimes or revealing secrets.
- **Humor** –Stories, mostly fictional, full of fun and excitement meant to entertain readers. Can be seen in stories from all genres.
- **Myth** -A legend or traditional narrative, often based on a historical event. The story reveals something about human behavior or the natural world, and often involves actions of gods.

Review Video: Literary Genres
Visit mometrix.com/academy and enter code: 587617

Drama

DRAMA

Dramas are texts that are written to be performed by people reading the lines or acting the stories out. They can also be presented as monologues (one character speaks), dialogues (two character speak to each other), or pantomimes (body movements are used instead of spoken words). Dramatic texts are called plays or **scripts**, and they are written differently than other texts.

TEXT STRUCTURE IN DRAMA

Plays are divided into **acts** (large units) and **scenes** (small sections inside acts) instead of chapters. There are also **stage directions**, which are instructions from the playwright about where items go, where actors should move, and what the characters should be doing during the scene. Stage directions are usually in italics to set them apart from other parts of the play. When it is time for a character in a play to speak, there will be **character tag** on the left side of the page which shows the name of the character (all letters of the name are capitalized) followed by a colon.

Here is an example of how a page from a play might look:

Title of Play

Act Number

Scene Number

The setting of the scene is being described here. The reader is being introduced to the characters and the things happening around them. Characters will enter speak to one another during the scene.

CHARACTER 1:

I am speaking. These are words I say. *(stage directions)* I am still speaking.

CHARACTER 2 *enters and does something.*

CHARACTER 2:

Now I am speaking. This is my dialogue.

DIALOGUE AND STAGE DIRECTIONS

Dialogue refers to what the characters say in a play when they are talking to each other, talking to themselves, or even talking to the audience. The type of speech, word choice, and accent a character uses is specific to the role he is playing. For example, a person cast to play a cowboy would have certain words in his vocabulary that a character from a big city in the North would not have.

A playwright also uses stage directions to make the play flow smoothly. Character interaction helps the viewer to understand the mood of the scene. If two characters are confrontational, the viewer is aware that there is some type of conflict occurring. Stage directions create order when all the characters are on stage together.

Soliloquy

A moment when a character is speaking alone on stage is called a **soliloquy**. Oftentimes characters reveal something personal or dramatic in soliloquies because no other characters in the play can hear them. of course, the audience is listening, so these are opportunities for the character to be one on one with the audience. Soliloquies play a large role in shaping a play or drama because they allow the audience to have first-hand knowledge of what a character is feeling or thinking without having the interference of the other characters in the play. They are a chance for a character to bare his or her soul to the world in general. This experience creates an intensity of feeling between the character and the audience that leads to greater understanding of the character's personal plight and the meaning of the play.

Organization of a Text

Introducing a Topic

When writing an informational or explanatory text, the author will need to introduce the topic that the text will be about. There are numerous strategies that can help improve the reader's comprehension of the subject. an author may choose to define key words that a reader may not be familiar with, classify information or compare and contrast it, or use a cause and effect relationship in the report. Charts and tables are extremely useful for displaying complicated information and the use of headings can help signify where certain information will be found. Multimedia devices, including video and audio, can also improve the way in which an author displays his material because they are appealing to the audience or reader.

Developing a Topic

To develop a topic in an informational or explanatory text, an author needs to use relevant facts that support details related to the main topic. The topic may be included in a topic sentence or opening statement and then followed by supporting details. Some of the supporting details should be concrete facts that have been researched and confirmed. Quotations of experts in the field of the topic are another good source for supporting material. Quoting experts gives variety and credence to a text. Examples, charts, and multimedia techniques can also be used to enhance the presentation, but these extras should not be used as a substitute for solid supporting details.

Example

Analyze the beginning of this informational text and tell what could be added to improve it.

> The journey of the salmon from salt water to fresh water to breed is one of the wonders of nature. This journey, called the salmon run, is difficult because the fish must swim upriver against the current. Some even leap up waterfalls as they make their way back to their original breeding grounds.

This seems like a good start to an informational text. The first sentence establishes the topic. It tells what the report is going to be about. It also includes two supporting details to tell more about the topic. This is one way to introduce and develop a topic in a report or other informational or explanatory text. What should come next are more supporting details and also sources for the information that is cited; a quotation from an authority of the salmon run would make the report stronger and give it credence. Some statistics, facts, figures about how many salmon make the run each year and how many survive would also be of interest.

Using Appropriate Transitions

When writing an informational or explanatory text it is important to use appropriate transitions that will clarify the relationships among ideas and concepts. For example, to show causality between ideas, use transition words or phrases, such as "therefore," "consequently," and "as a result of." to show comparison or contrast relationships, words such as "however," "on the other hand," "but," "in contrast," and "similarly" should be used. Transition words and expressions to introduce examples include "for example, "for instance," "namely" and "that is." the order of importance can also be shown through transitions, such as "at first," "former," "latter," "primarily" and "second."

Importance of Using Precise Language and Domain-Specific Vocabulary

When writing informational or explanatory texts it is of utmost importance to use precise language and domain-specific vocabulary to explain your main idea and supporting details. Generalized vocabulary will not help the audience grasp the points that you are attempting to make because they will not accurately reflect your main idea and supporting details. Domain-specific vocabulary is important to use because it will accurately describe or explain the ideas or processes that are central to your text. When you research a subject, make sure to familiarize yourself with any vocabulary that is involved in its explanation. Use context clues, dictionaries, or, if necessary, a technical dictionary to decode any words that you are not familiar with. Also include definitions of domain-specific vocabulary in your text to enlighten readers.

Establishing and Maintaining a Formal Style

When writing an informational or explanatory text it is important to establish and maintain a formal style of writing. Do not use a colloquial or casual tone. It is necessary to use the third person and to make the sentences longer and more complex. It is also important not to use contractions when you write. A formal style announces that the writer is serious about his or her subject and wants to write an objective paper. This can be done by keeping the main ideas and supporting details clear, to the point, but as complex as they need to be. A formal style also means that the writer will not include a personal opinion that is not justified.

Example

Discuss why the following excerpt is an example of formal writing.

> Richard Spruce found his life's work in the jungles of South America. Spruce grew up in a part of England that was filled with plants growing wild and free. His love of plants developed early. When he read a book about the Amazon jungle in Brazil, he decided to go there to study the area's plant life.

This is a good example of formal writing. It is objective and unbiased. The author uses the third person perspective, which formal writing is supposed to do. He sets out his main idea in the initial topic sentence, and then gives good supporting details. His sentences are somewhat complex and varied. He does not use any contractions, which are not used in formal writing, and the language is not colloquial or casual. The style of writing matches the subject. At the same time, the writing is not dull; the reader is intrigued and wants to learn more. Formal writing does not have to be uninteresting.

Importance of a Concluding Statement

A concluding statement or section that follows from and supports the information or explanation is important to a text because the conclusion helps to focus the important points in a text and also provides closure to the reader or audience. A good conclusion attempts to sum up the passage and any conclusions that the author makes so that the audience feels they have received a logical ending to the text. an effective conclusion gives the passage the weight it needs to have an effect. The conclusion should not make the reader feel that there is more information to follow, but rather set the tone for the ending of the topic.

Organizational Patterns

When writing there are a variety of ways that an author can choose to organize their text. It is important for them to choose the pattern that best presents their information, as not all patterns will work for every piece of writing. Some examples are:

Advantage/Disadvantage

The author chooses a topic or concept and addresses both the advantages and disadvantages (or pros and cons) of the subject. in this type of text, the author is not trying to persuade their audience to choose a side, but rather, to inform the reader of all the possible positive and negative effects.

Cause and Effect

The author will write about relationship between two events that occur, where the second event occurs as a result of the first.

For example, a text may discuss a school policy stating that when a student is late to school too many times, they receive a detention. Later in the text, we might see a student repeatedly arriving late to school, after which he is given a detention. in this example, the **cause** is the student being late to school, and the **effect** is the student receiving a detention.

Classification

The author chooses a topic and divides it into smaller parts or groups in order to discuss them individually. These types of texts address how parts work within a whole, or what characteristics can be used to classify a given subject or concept.

Chronological Order

the author organizes the progression of events based upon when they occurred and what was included in each step of the story. By organizing the text in this way, the author presents all necessary information about the six questions readers can ask to help themselves understand the text: who, what, when, where, why, and how.

Compare and Contrast

The author will show similarities and differences between items or events.

For example, the author may write about cats and dogs. They might start by giving a brief description of the two. Then they will want to point out all of the similarities, such as; they both have tails, and both are kept as pets. Next, they will explain the differences, such as; dogs are canines, while cats are felines. They will try to provide as much detail as possible about both the similarities and the differences.

Definition

Authors introduce a concept or word and then explain or describe it. This type of text often included examples that will help the reader gain understanding of what is presumably a new concept for them.

Inductive / Deductive

Authors organize ideas from general to specific or specific to general. If ideas are organized **inductively**, they are arranged from specific facts to general conclusions. If ideas are organized from general conclusions to specific facts, they are organized **deductively**. A reader can make a logical assumption about a topic based on the facts that are presented in the text.

For example, in these two sentences the ideas are organized deductively, from general to specific.

> Many canoers use the lake in the summer. Jeff learned how to canoe last summer, and is on his way to the lake now.

The idea that "Many canoers use the lake in the summer" is a general idea. The facts that Jeff already knows how to canoe and is headed to the lake are specific to him as a character.

Order of Importance

The author puts the information in the text in order of what is most important. Order of importance can be either increasing or decreasing, depending on how the writer wants to structure the work.

Proposition and Support

The author states a proposition that they believe to be true, and then provides support for that proposition in the paper. The topics that use this type of structure are generally things that reader might feel uncertain about or might not already have an opinion about. The support that the author gives for the proposition should include facts, statistics, logic, and reasoning. The more hard-evidence an author can give the reader, the better it will help convince them to see things from the author's point of view.

Identifying Organizational Strategies

Example

Explain which organization pattern would be the best choice for this writer and why.

> Sara is writing a report on sea turtles. She has researched the various dangers that they face: their predators, the difficulties they encounter in their life cycle starting with their birth, their migration to the ocean, and the dangers that await them as they mature. She is unsure of how to organize her report.

A cause and effect order would seem to be the best idea for Sara because she would be able to identify the causes and effects of the dangers that sea turtles encounter. She could organize the report so that each paragraph deals with a different threat, using headings to identify what would be in each section. A chart would also be useful because it puts the same information in a clear format so that readers would be able to refer to it. She might also consider using a video showing baby turtles migrating towards the open sea, which would give her audience an even greater understanding of the turtles' plight.

Example 2

Identify the text structure that is used in the following sentences:

> Madison and her brother Jake used to live on a wind-torn island in the Chesapeake Bay. Last year they moved to Baltimore, a city in Maryland. Next summer they plan to visit the island where they grew up.

Chronological order is used as a text structure in the example sentences, as they are organized according to the passage of time. Note that each sentence refers to a point in time. The first sentence refers to where the siblings lived in the past. The second sentence refers to the siblings' move to Baltimore last year. The final sentence refers to what the siblings plan to do in the future. By referring to a specific place in time, the reader can see what occurred in the story during that time period. an author will often use flashback to indicate what happened in the past, and foreshadowing to give the reader a glimpse of what may occur in the future.

Example 3

Identify the text structure that is used in the following sentences:

> Three cousins lived in the same small town. One day the cousins decided to journey together to enter a singing contest across the country. The cousins won the contest and made their hometown fans proud.

The information in the story can be organized according to the passage of time, called chronological order. The story will start based in the cousins' hometown, to give some background on where the cousins come from. Subsequent events in the story will occur over time based on the cousins' motivations due to their background. The story will end by referring back to how far the cousins have come from their small-town roots.

Author's Purpose and Message

Author's Purpose

The author's purpose is going to be their reason for writing the text. As the reader reads a text, they should always try to figure out the author's purpose for writing as this will help them to better understand the message that the author is trying to convey.

Informational Texts

- Inform the reader on a topic that they previously knew nothing about, such as many non-fiction texts.
- For example, an informative paper on early Native American Indian tribes would detail where Native American Indians lived, what types of foods they ate, how they bartered for goods, and other aspects of their culture.

Persuasive Texts

- Influence the reader to think a certain way about a topic, calling them to action or pointing them toward resources that would help them to learn more about the topic.
- A **Proposition and Support** paper would be an example of this, where an author gives their opinion and then tries to convince the reader to see something from their point of view.
- For example, an author may try to persuade the reader that waterparks are the best place to go in the summer when it is hot outside. The author would present information about waterparks and explain *why* they are good places to visit.

Expressive Texts

- Express the author or speaker's opinion or emotions about a topic. Generally, expressive texts include descriptive words to clearly show the reader how the author or speaker feels.
- For example, the author of a poem may think that compassion is an important quality in a person, and they may write a poem in which the speaker discusses how compassion is what binds all people together.

Entertaining Texts

- Entertain the reader, such as in most fictional texts.
- For example, Wilson Rawls, the author of *Where the Red Fern Grows* entertains his readers with the adventures of a young boy named Billy and his two hound dogs, Old Dan and Little Ann.

Review Video: Understanding the Author's Intent
Visit mometrix.com/academy and enter code: 511819

Example 1

Read the following sentence. State the author's point in writing the sentence, whether it is to inform, persuade, express an opinion, or entertain:

> The rollercoaster reached a peak and paused for a second, before gliding down the other side of the hill with a roar.

The purpose of the sentence is to entertain the reader. The author does not state his or her opinion on the topic, and the sentence doesn't inform the reader about an important topic. The sentence does not persuade the reader to accept a certain point of view, and is instead meant to entertain the reader by giving them the feeling they might get from riding an exciting roller coaster.

Notice that the text describes an event, rather than an issue or conflict. The event is part of a larger tale, where a series of events occur to form an entire story. The reader may notice that the author uses descriptive words to present the setting, such as gliding and roar. The reader can better picture a story when the setting is clearly presented.

Example 2

Read the following sentence and state the author's point in writing the sentence, whether it is to inform, entertain, persuade, or state an opinion:

> The new student handbook makes it against the rules to wear roller skates inside the school buildings.

The purpose of this sentence is to inform the reader. The sentence does not state an opinion on the topic, nor is it meant to entertain the reader. The sentence also does not persuade the reader to accept a certain point of view. The sentence gives information to the reader that they need to know in order to avoid breaking the rules.

Example 3

Read the following sentence from the *City of Ember* by Jeanne DuPrau and state the author's purpose in writing the sentence: whether it is to inform, entertain, persuade, or state an opinion:

> Lina looked out at the lighted streets spreading away in every direction, the streets she knew so well. She loved her city, worn out and crumbling though it was

The purpose of the sentence is to entertain the reader. The sentence does not tell the reader important information about a specific topic, it is simply used as part of a greater fictional story meant for entertainment. The sentence does not persuade the reader to accept a certain point of view, nor does it state an opinion.

When an author wishes to persuade the reader to accept a certain point of view, evidence is used to back-up a claim. If the author wants to state an opinion, that opinion is included within the text. Sentences that are meant to inform contain facts that the reader needs to know and are not often found in fictional stories.

Determining the Purpose of a Text

When reading, the reader should always determine the purpose of a text. to do so, ask yourself what effect the writing has on you. Does the text try to explain or persuade you of something? Perhaps the text is making an appeal to your emotions. The signs that a text is attempting to persuade you include an author offering an opinion and explaining why she thinks this way. On the other hand, if a text is simply informative, it will have many facts that will give details about an event, person, or idea without trying to persuade you of anything. Manuals that come with equipment are clearly not persuasive, simply instructive.

Example

Explain the purpose of the passage below.

> No pop star should earn extreme amounts of money simply for singing songs. Entertainers should be allowed to earn up to one million dollars per year and no more. The money they are given for just entertaining the masses could better be put to better use. There are many people in our country struggling to provide for their families despite working hard, and it's unfair that entertainers make so much by doing so little.

The purpose of the excerpt is to convince people that the income of pop singers should be restricted. This is clearly what the author wants to happen. He gives an argument for capping their income when he says "the money… could be put to better use." He uses reasons that he feels are important to convince people, stating that "there are many people in our country struggling." the author does not urge a particular way to make this happen, just that an income cap should be enforced.

Reading Persuasive Texts

When an author's purpose is to persuade, readers need to look for misleading, exaggerated or contradictory statements. These types of statements can show up if the author's opinion, instead of fact, is shown in the text.

Fact and Opinion

When deciding whether information is fact or opinion, a reader needs to look at whether or not the information is well-accepted by experts, in addition to being backed-up by outside sources. A fact is something that is true, regardless of what the author thinks, on the contrary, an opinion is what the author thinks, without regard to evidence to back-up that claim.

For example, in a paper about caves, a fact may read: Extensive cave systems run through the soft limestone of Central Texas. An opinion may read: caving, also called spelunking, is an enjoyable recreational activity. It is a fact that caves run throughout Central Texas, but it is the author's opinion that spelunking is an enjoyable recreational activity.

Author's Use of Print and Graphic Features

Print and Graphic Features

An author may show information in a chart, a graph, in paragraph format, or as a list. Information may also be shown in a picture or a diagram. The way an author chooses to show information is often based on the purpose of the text and the audience that the text is meant to reach.

A reader may be asked to answer questions based on the graphic by itself, how the graphic relates to the text, or how the text would best be shown in a graphic form.

Cause and Effect Graphic Organizers

Often used to map the **elements of a story**. A reader might read a story about a string of events and then be asked to correctly fill in either the **cause** or **effect** of an event in the story.

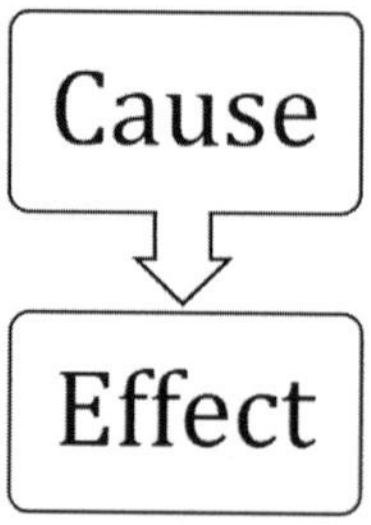

Review Video: Graphic Organizers
Visit mometrix.com/academy and enter code: 665513

Example

Read the following excerpt from *Holes* by Louis Sachar and decide what effect Stanley's letter has on his mother:

> Dear Stanley,
>
> It was wonderful to hear from you. Your letter made me feel like one of the other moms who can afford to send their kids to summer camp. I know it's not the same, but I am very proud of you for trying to make the best of a bad situation.

A **cause and effect** graphic organizer for this excerpt might look something like this:

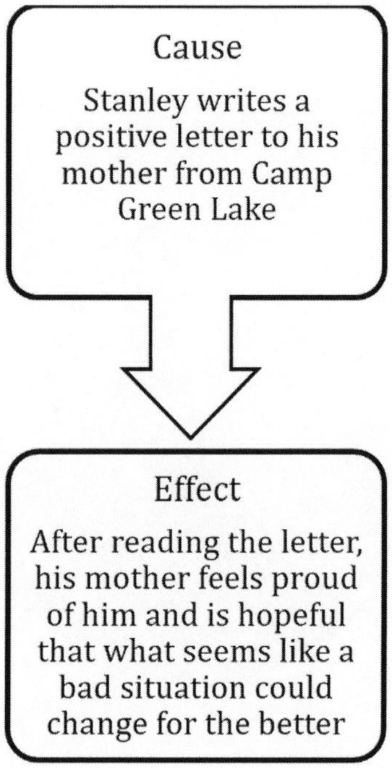

LINE GRAPHS

Used for measuring general **trends over time**. For example, this line graph shows an overall upward trend in the amount of candy bars sold for four weeks.

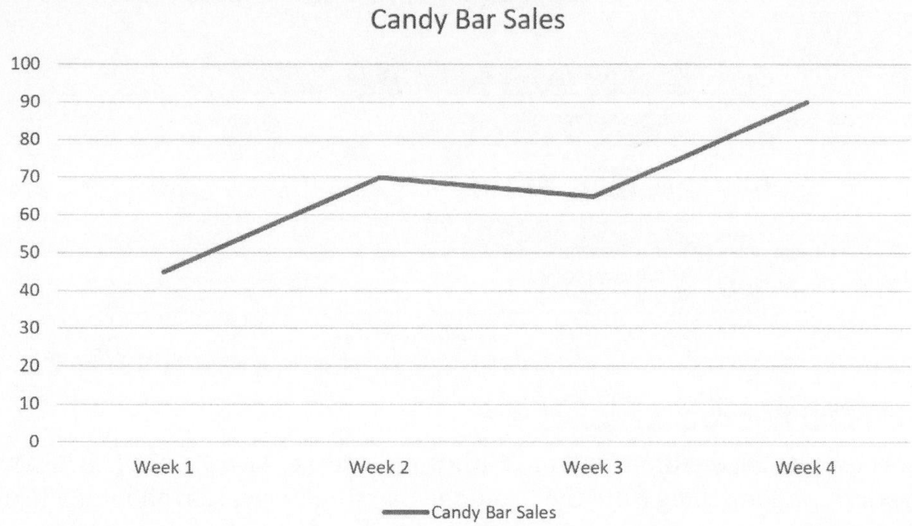

Circle Graphs (Also Called Pie Charts)

Used to represent information that can be shown as **parts of a whole**. For example, this graph shows the results of people being asked about their favorite color:

Favorite Color

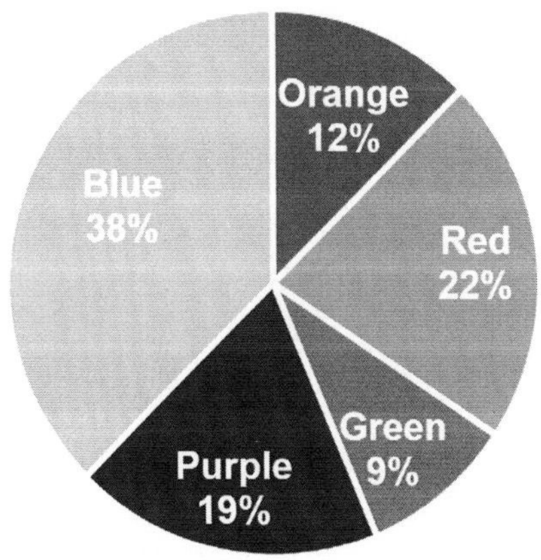

Bar Graphs

Used to illustrate sets of numerical data. The bar graph is one of the most common visual representations of information. For example, this graph is a different way of representing the same results as those in the circle graph:

Favorite Color

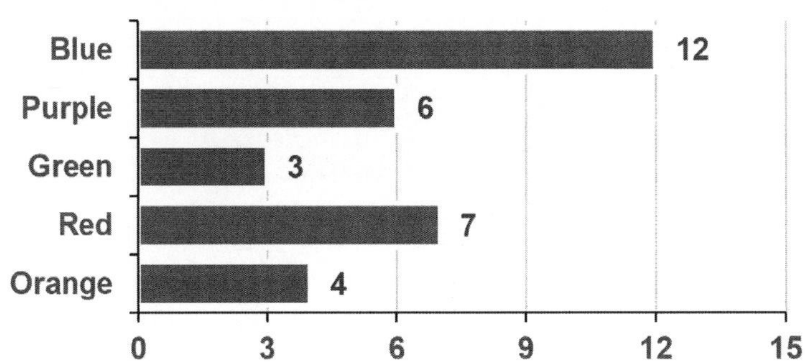

Illustrations and Photographs

Authors may choose to include **illustrations** or **photographs** (or both) with their texts. These two image types both show something from the text or give more information about the text.

Illustrations are drawings of an object. They may be based on reality, or they may represent an artist's abstract idea. For example, this is an illustration of a 1903 automobile:

Photographs are pictures of objects. They are generally extremely realistic, and most often show an object as it actually existed at that moment in time. For example, this is a photograph of a 1917 automobile:

Both illustrations and photographs give the reader another way to relate to and understand the text. The reader may be asked how the image relates to the text, what type of caption the image should be given, or why the author chose to include the image with the text.

Diagrams

Used to show information in a visual way. There are many different types of diagrams, including:

Diagrams that show the parts of an object, how they work together, or how they should be put together. This is an example of a diagram which shows how gears turn together:

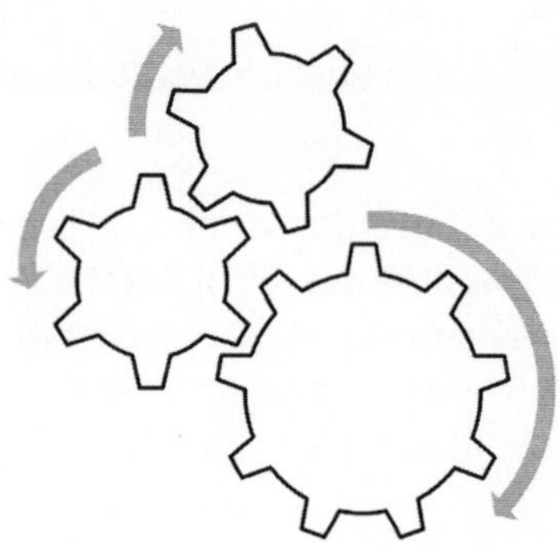

Diagrams that show how information is related are called **Venn Diagrams**. These are ways to visually see the way in which two different ideas overlap. This is an example of a Venn Diagram comparing cats and dogs:

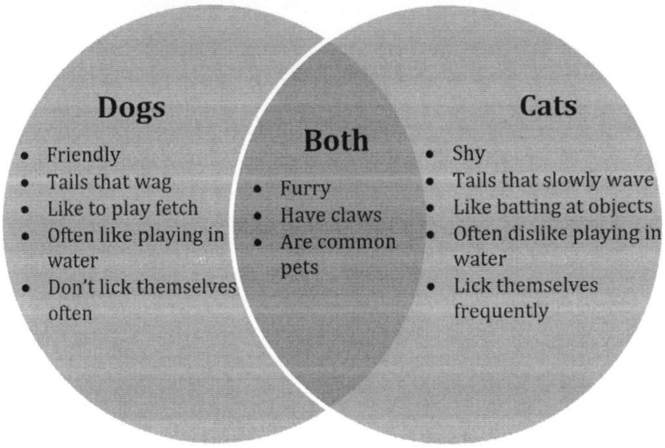

Author's Use of Figurative Language

Literal and Figurative Language

Many types of text use both **literal language**, which means just what it says, and **figurative language**, which allows the writer to expand the way in which he or she uses language. When an author uses figurative language, she connects things in an exaggerated and non-literal way in order to create a memorable image, which helps to describe a situation in a new way for the reader.

Review Video: Figurative Language Visit mometrix.com/academy and enter code: 584902

Imagery

Imagery is the use of **descriptive language** to add life or feeling to a work of literature. Many authors add literary and sound devices to create vivid pictures in the minds of their readers. Most of the time, imagery is thought to be one of the best ways to help readers fully understand and remember a work.

The most common forms of imagery are those that appeal to the sense of sight and sound. Imagery that appeals to the sense of sight, or **visual imagery**, helps the reader picture an event in their mind, usually by including specific details in the text that are not strictly necessary for the purpose of the story, but allow the reader to more easily envision the scene. Some common forms of figurative language that help create visual imagery include.

Metaphor

- Puts one idea in place of another to draw a parallel between the two ideas.
- For example, an author might write "Her room was a pigsty," to compare a person's bedroom to a dirty spot where pigs sleep.

Simile

- Shows similarity between two ideas or objects, using the words "**like**" or "**as**"
- For example, an author might write "The princess is as beautiful as a rose" to compare the appearance of a woman to a beautiful flower.

Symbolism

- Using one object to stand for something else.
- For example, an author may include a flag flying high throughout a story to show pride in the characters' country and to represent the idea of patriotism.

Hyperbole

- An extreme exaggeration of an idea.
- For example, a character might say "I'm starving to death!" to show that they are really hungry. Most of the time a character who says this is not literally going to die from hunger, they are just ready for a snack.

Irony

- Uses sarcasm or humor (usually with an emphasis on the opposite) to show difference from literal meaning.
- For example, if a character says "Well today must be my lucky day!" after they left their homework on the kitchen table, they are being ironic. The irony used here helps show that it is definitely *not* the character's lucky day.

Personification

- Gives life or human characteristics to an inanimate object
- For example, if an author writes "The trees whispered to each other across the wide blue sky," they are using personification to help the reader imagine the scene. Trees are not human beings, so they do not whisper, but the image created in the reader stands out more than a literal description would.

Example 1

Based on current knowledge, identify whether metaphor, simile, or hyperbole is used in this sentence:

> The chiming bell was a beacon of hope for the downtrodden villagers.

A **metaphor** is used in this sentence to draw a parallel between "the chiming bell" and "a beacon of hope." the bell is being compared to something else in the sentence, which indicates the use of metaphor or simile, but the reader knows that the sentence does not contain a simile, because the words like and as are not used to show the comparison. The sentence also does not contain an exaggeration of facts, so the reader can see that hyperbole is not used.

Example 2

Based on experience, determine the meaning of the idiom in the following sentence:

> Jared **hung his head** after viewing his score on the test and realizing that he had not studied the material long enough.

In the example, the phrase 'hung his head' is an **idiom** that means to look down with shame. By reading the rest of the sentence, the reader can see that the character did not study enough, which would lead him to be upset about his score on the test. Idioms can be figured out through the use of context clues, but are also learned through experience with the language.

EXAMPLE 3

Discuss the kind of figurative language used in the following poem by the Scottish poet Robert Burns:

> O my luve's like a red, red rose
> That's newly sprung in June;
> O my luve's like the melodie
> That's sweetly played in tune.

The poet uses **similes** to create an image in this poem. The two similes here occur when the speaker says that his love is "**like** a red, red rose" and that she is also "**like** the melodie." These are examples of similes because they use the comparing word 'like' to compare two things. They are not metaphors because metaphors do not use the comparing words 'like' or 'as.' the poem paints an image of the speaker's love by comparing her to a red rose that has newly sprung and a melody that is sweetly played.

EXAMPLE 4

Read the following excerpt from "The Raven" by Edgar Allan Poe, identify the metaphor, and discuss how it impacts the text:

> And the raven, never flitting, still is sitting, still is sitting
> On the pallid bust of Pallas just above my chamber door;
> And his eyes have all the seeming of a demon's that is dreaming

One **metaphor** in the excerpt from "The Raven" by Edgar Allan Poe is: "And his eyes have all the seeming of a demon's that is dreaming"

The metaphor compares the raven's eyes with a demon, which shows that the speaker thinks there is evil in the bird. The metaphor helps contribute to the overall tone of the poem and the reader's understanding of how the speaker views the bird.

EXAMPLE 5

Read the excerpt from a poem by William Blake and describe what form of figurative language it uses.

> The wild winds weep,
> And the night is a-cold;
> Come hither, sleep,
> And my griefs unfold.

This poem contains several examples of **personification**. in the poem, the speaker says "The wild winds weep," thereby giving the winds the human characteristic of weeping. Later it says "Come hither, sleep," which is another use of personification asking that sleep to go somewhere as though it were a person. The poem gives the winds and sleep human characteristics. This is the definition of personification. It is not an example of simile because there is no comparison using the words "as" or "like." It is not a metaphor because there is no comparison between two things sharing a similar quality. and it is not an example of hyperbole because there is no exaggeration. The poem does contain some alliteration, however; the repetition of the letter "w" in "wild winds weep" qualifies as alliteration, which is another literary technique.

Sound Devices

Sound devices allow authors to add another level to their texts by tapping into the spoken part of language. Imagery that appeals to the sense of hearing, or **auditory imagery**. Authors may use many sound devices to create meaning and help readers understand them better, including

Onomatopoeia

- Appeals to the reader's sense of hearing by using words that copy the noises objects or people make, like sound effects.
- For example, an author might write "The soccer ball whooshed across the field into the goalie's net, scoring the winning point!" The word "whooshed" is an onomatopoeia because it mimics the sound of air moving quickly. Because the writer chose to include an onomatopoeia, the reader is able to better picture the action in the sentence.

Reading Practice Test #1

Questions 1 – 12 pertain to the following short story:

A World of White: The Iditarod Trail

(1) Imagine clinging desperately to your sled as brutal winds batter your body. The path ahead appears and disappears like a mirage, frequently obscured by blowing curtains of snow. You are freezing and sweating at the same time. Your throat burns with thirst, and your body aches with fatigue. You know your dogs must feel it too, so you encourage them to press on to the next checkpoint. All around you, the world is endless, empty, and white. Welcome to the Iditarod Trail.

(2) Alaska's Iditarod Trail is the world's most famous sled dog racing venue. But the trail is older than the sport of sled dog racing. In fact, the Iditarod Trail was first established in the early 1900s, during the Alaskan gold rush. In those days, dog teams were used for work, hauling thousands of pounds of gold from landlocked Iditarod to the port of Anchorage. But in faraway Nome, also known for gold, six-year-old George Allen had the idea to put together a race to see whose sled dogs were fastest, and the sport of sled dog racing was born.

(3) Though the Iditarod Trail race is the most famous race in the sport of sled dog racing, the first race along the trail was actually a race to save lives. In 1925, a diphtheria outbreak began in Nome. To prevent an epidemic that could kill thousands, doctors were desperate for the vaccine serum, but the closest serum was in Anchorage. The train ran from Anchorage to the village of Nenana, but that was still 674 miles from Nome. A cry for help was sent by the doctors, and in the midst of the blizzards and windstorms of January, the call was answered. Twenty brave mushers drove their dogs in a frantic relay, carrying 300,000 bottles of serum from Nenana to Nome. They followed the Iditarod Trail.

(4) Dog sledding, or "mushing," became quite popular after that heroic journey, but by the 1960s, it had lost popularity and the Iditarod Trail had been largely forgotten. There were a few lovers of mushing, however, who worked tirelessly to reestablish the Iditarod Trail and create a new sled dog race that used the trail as its course. The first official race was held in 1967 to celebrate the centennial of the purchase of Alaska from Russia. The race involved 58 drivers who mushed 56 miles in two days. This race was a success, but the popularity and future of the Iditarod Trail was still in question.

(5) In March of 1973, the first Anchorage to Nome Iditarod Trail race was organized and held. This race was much longer than previous races, covering more than 1,000 miles—the whole Iditarod Trail. Thirty-four mushers began the race, but only 22 were able to finish. After the 1973 race, the popularity of the Iditarod Trail finally grew and was firmly established. In 1978, the Iditarod Trail became a National Historic Trail.

(6) The modern Iditarod Trail race is open to mushers over 18 years old who have qualified in a recognized race of 200 miles or more. For younger mushers between 14 and 18 years old, the Junior Iditarod offers a 130-mile version of the race. Many

Junior Iditarod participants go on to compete in the Iditarod Trail race, as the Junior Iditarod is good practice for the grueling trek of the main race. All mushers must prepare for the race extensively, often for months before the race. Many mushers run their dogs more than 1,500 miles in preparation, giving them experience in all types of weather and terrain.

(7) To enter the Iditarod Trail race, participants must pay an entrance fee. Then they must travel to Anchorage with their dogs. In Anchorage, they attend a mushers' banquet where they are given their racing order numbers. Afterwards, all participating dogs are checked by a veterinarian and marked by race officials to prevent dog switching mid-race, which is not allowed. The dogs are even drug tested at the beginning and at checkpoints throughout the race to prevent cheating! Finally, the sleds and equipment are checked. Then participants are ready to start the race.

(8) On the morning of the Iditarod Trail race, mushers leave Anchorage in their assigned racing order. They are sent out one at a time, at two-minute intervals. For more than a week—sometimes up to three weeks—they travel throughout Alaska, stopping at designated checkpoints all along the Iditarod Trail as they make their way to Nome. When all participants have reached Nome, another mushers' banquet is held. Awards are given, and everyone is applauded for their achievement. Win or lose, the mushers know that only the toughest of the tough have what it takes to finish the race and conquer the great Iditarod Trail.

1. What does the simile in paragraph 1 describe?

a. The snow
b. The path
c. The musher's throat
d. The dogs

2. What does "landlocked" mean in paragraph 2?

a. Barricaded by hills
b. Built underground
c. Not on a waterway
d. In the mountains

3. What two cities are on the ends of the Iditarod Trail?

a. Anchorage and Nome
b. Nome and Nenana
c. Iditarod and Anchorage
d. Nenana and Iditarod

4. What is the author's main purpose in writing this article?

a. To encourage mushers to race on the Iditarod Trail
b. To inform the reader about the 1925 diphtheria outbreak
c. To describe the terrain of Alaska
d. To educate the reader about the Iditarod Trail

5. In paragraph 3, which words best convey the feelings of the doctors in Nome in 1925?

a. "Epidemic" and "diphtheria"
b. "Blizzards" and "windstorms"
c. "Brave" and "frantic relay"
d. "Desperate" and "cry for help"

6. Why did the author choose to write this article in third-person point of view?

a. Historical overviews are best written in third person
b. The author has never been to Alaska
c. Third person is the required point of view in nonfiction writing
d. This article is not written in third-person point of view

7. In what year did the Iditarod Trail become a National Historic Trail?

a. 1967
b. 1973
c. 1978
d. 1981

8. Which of the following is the best summary of the history of the Iditarod Trail race?

a. After the Iditarod Trail became a National Historic Trail, the race became more popular, and today many mushers participate each year
b. After a slow start in 1967, the Iditarod Trail race became firmly established in 1973, and it continues in popularity today
c. In the first race in 1973, 34 mushers began the race, but only 22 were able to finish, proving that the race was just too hard
d. Mushers between 14 and 18 years of age can race in the Junior Iditarod, while those over 18 can participate in the main race if they qualify

9. How is this article organized?

a. Chronologically
b. Geographically
c. Randomly
d. Spatially

10. Which of the following is a supporting detail in this article?

a. Alaska's Iditarod Trail is the world's most famous sled dog racing venue
b. After the heroic journey of 1925, mushing became more popular
c. Some mushers run their dogs over 1,500 miles to prepare for the race
d. There are specific requirements to enter the Iditarod Trail race

11. What do participants receive at the first mushers' banquet?

a. Awards
b. Racing order numbers
c. Supplies
d. Trail maps

12. What is the interval used to separate mushers as they begin the Iditarod Trail race?

a. Five minutes
b. One minute
c. Ten minutes
d. Two minutes

Questions 13 –21 pertain to the following story:

The Right Thing to Do

Characters *(in order of appearance)*:

JESSICA—a sixth-grade girl, Amy's friend

GROUP OF FRIENDS—a group of sixth-grade girls

AMY—a sixth-grade girl, Jessica's friend

SALES CLERK—a clerk in the store Amy and Jessica visit

Scene 1

(1) *Jessica stands with a group of friends on the school steps. The group is chatting and laughing. Amy approaches from stage right.*

(2) AMY: Jessica! Jessica!

(3) JESSICA: *(turning away from her friends and taking a step toward Amy)* Hi, Amy. What's up?

(4) AMY: I'm headed to the mall, and I thought you might want to come.

(5) JESSICA: Why me? I thought we weren't friends anymore.

(6) AMY: *(waving her hand and shaking her head)* That old fight? Ancient history. So ... do you want to come or not?

(7) JESSICA: *(glancing back at her friends)* Sure. I'll come. Just give me a minute.

(8) *Jessica runs back and talks with her friends for a moment, then rejoins Amy. Amy and Jessica exit stage right.*

Scene 2

(9) *Amy and Jessica are looking at a shelf full of lipstick in a cosmetics store in the mall.*

(10) AMY: Look at this one, Jess. Don't you just love this color? *(She picks up a lipstick tube.)*

(11) JESSICA: It's nice, but I like this one better. *(She picks up a different tube of lipstick.)*

(12) *A sales clerk enters from stage left.*

(13) SALES CLERK: *(stopping by the girls)* Can I help you ladies find something?

(14) AMY: Oh, no. We're just looking.

(15) JESSICA: Thank you, though.

(16) SALES CLERK: Okay. Well, let me know if you need anything. *(He/she exits stage right.)*

(17) AMY: So, which one are you going to get?

(18) JESSICA: *(looking at the floor and shaking her head)* I'm not getting one. They're a little spendy for me. Besides, I'm saving up for something special.

(19) AMY: *(laughing)* Who said anything about money? *(She slips her favorite lipstick into her pocket.)* I didn't ask you which one you were going to buy. I asked which one you were going to get. So, which one will it be?

(20) JESSICA: But—but—that's stealing!

(21) AMY: Look at all these tubes of lipstick. They'll never miss a couple.

(22) JESSICA: *(looking around nervously)* What if that sales clerk comes back and catches us?

(23) AMY: You worry too much. *(She picks up two tubes of lipstick.)* Now, was this the one you liked? Or was it this one? Never mind. We'll take them both. *(She slips them both into her pocket.)*

(24) JESSICA: Amy! This is wrong. We shouldn't be doing this.

(25) AMY: *(glaring at Jessica)* Do you even want to be my friend again? It sure doesn't sound like it.

(26) JESSICA: Of course I want to be your friend. It's just—

(27) AMY: Then come on. Let's go. *(She starts to walk away, and then turns and looks back.)* Are you coming?

(28) JESSICA: Fine. *(She follows Amy.)* But what if the alarm goes off?

(29) AMY: For a couple of tubes of lipstick? Not gonna happen. Now, follow me. And for heaven's sake, don't look so nervous.

(30) *The girls exit stage right.*

Scene 3

(31) *Jessica reenters the cosmetics store from stage right. She stops at the shelf of lipsticks and looks around. The sales clerk enters from stage left.*

(32) JESSICA: Excuse me ...

(33) SALES CLERK: *(stopping)* Did you need help with something?

(34) JESSICA: Yes. *(She looks at the floor.)* My friend who was just with me, um, she took—well, actually, she stole three tubes of lipstick. I'm not okay with that. So, um, I wanted to pay for them.

(35) SALES CLERK: That's impressive. I've never seen that happen before. And kids take stuff from this store all the time. What made you come back?

(36) JESSICA: *(shrugging)* I don't know. I guess it was just the right thing to do.

13. In paragraph 6, what does Amy mean when she calls her fight with Jessica "ancient history"?

a. It happened thousands of years ago
b. It happened in history class
c. Amy has totally forgotten about the fight
d. They were arguing about events in ancient history

14. What is the setting for Scene 1?

a. The school steps
b. The mall
c. A cosmetics store
d. Amy's house

15. What is the setting for Scene 2 and Scene 3?

a. The school steps
b. Jessica's house
c. A cosmetics store
d. Amy's house

16. Which scene contains the climax of this play?

a. Scene 1
b. Scene 2
c. Scene 3
d. All of the above

17. In paragraph 29, why is the word "gonna" considered acceptable?

a. It shows Amy's pattern of slang speech
b. It is always acceptable in written English
c. It is a different language spoken by Amy
d. It is not acceptable; it is a misspelling

18. In paragraph 6, what type of figurative language is used when Amy says "ancient history"?

a. Metaphor
b. Simile
c. Personification
d. Hyperbole

19. Which of the following best describes the overall tone of this play?

a. Formal
b. Conversational
c. Classical
d. Musical

20. What is the underlying theme of this play?

a. Amy and Jessica are best friends
b. Doing the right thing is always a good decision
c. It is okay to steal if you are not caught
d. Shopping for cosmetics increases peer pressure

21. Which of the following is the best summary of this play?

a. Jessica leaves her other friends to be friends with Amy again, and she and Amy go to the mall
b. Amy teaches Jessica how to steal lipstick without getting caught, being a bad influence on Jessica
c. Jessica agrees to go to the mall with Amy, but when Amy steals lipstick, Jessica goes back to pay for it
d. Jessica thinks stealing is wrong, and she thinks Amy is a bad influence because she is a thief

Questions 22 – 36 pertain to the following two short stories:

The Talent Show

(1) The first notes floated from the piano. Megan smiled, warm and excited beneath the glaring stage lights. This was her moment. She had practiced. She had prepared. She was ready. As the introduction ended, Megan opened her mouth and began to sing.

(2) The song flowed along, and Megan relaxed, scanning the faces of the audience. But somewhere in the middle of the second verse, her mind suddenly went blank. The music went on, but the words were gone. Megan's smile faded. She stood silently with her mouth hanging open. When the music finally trickled to a stop, Megan ran from the stage.

(3) In a cramped dressing room backstage, Megan buried her face in her hands. She had wanted so much to win this talent show. Tears seeped between her fingers. Her confidence and pride and excitement had been replaced by utter disappointment. She felt a hand on her shoulder and lifted her damp face.

(4) "Ella and Kaylee are here," Megan's mom said, giving her shoulder a quick squeeze.

(5) Ella and Kaylee, Megan's two best friends, pulled folding chairs over to face Megan. She looked at them forlornly.

(6) "I'm a total failure," she moaned.

(7) Ella and Kaylee exchanged glances. Kaylee reached out and squeezed Megan's hand.

(8) "What are you talking about?" Kaylee said. "That first verse was some of your best singing ever."

(9) "Thanks," Megan said. "But the problem is that the first verse is all I sang. Then I totally bombed. I can't believe I forgot the words after all that practice."

(10) "You didn't totally bomb," Ella said. "You just forgot the words. That happens to everybody. Besides, don't the pros say you should leave your audience wanting more?"

(11) "I guess so," Megan admitted.

(12) "Well, trust me," Ella said. "I guarantee they wanted more—like the rest of the song! You probably did, too."

(13) Megan smiled a little. "So, you guys don't think I'm a total dork for forgetting the words?"

(14) "Of course not," Kaylee said. "Forgetting the words doesn't make you a dork. It just makes you human. And you're still the most talented person I know."

(15) Ella nodded in agreement. Megan pulled Ella and Kaylee into a quick hug. Then she wiped her eyes and managed a genuine smile.

(16) "I'm so lucky to have best friends like you two," Megan said. "It's nice to know that you'll be my friends forever, no matter what!"

The Tournament

(1) Looking for a hole in the defense, Scott dribbled the ball, shifting it from hand to hand. A trickle of sweat ran down his back. No one was open. There were only seconds left on the clock, and Scott knew he had a difficult decision to make.

(2) The other team was leading by two points, and Scott was just outside the three-point line. If he could make the shot, the Eagles would be state champions again. But if he missed ... Scott didn't want to think about that. He knew what he had to do.

(3) It was a classic jump shot. The ball left his hands and sailed toward the basket in a perfect arc. The crowd, the other players, the whole stadium seemed frozen in time. All eyes were on the ball as it struck the rim and bounced off. The buzzer blared. The game was over. Scott had missed, and the Eagles had lost.

(4) Scott stood like a statue on the court as people surged around him. Elated family members swarmed the winning team. Teammates hugged and slapped each other on the back. Even Scott's own teammates joined in the celebration.

(5) Suddenly, Scott felt himself being hoisted unsteadily onto the shoulders of his friends. Over the loudspeaker, the announcer proclaimed that Scott had been named the most valuable player of the championship game. Everyone cheered, and the Eagles took a victory lap with Scott on their shoulders. Finally, Scott's friends put him back on solid ground.

(6) Scott was bewildered. He was the one who missed the most important shot of the game. How could anyone call him the most valuable player? He didn't feel very valuable at the moment. Scott approached Coach Travis.

(7) "Coach," Scott said, "there must be some mistake. I can't be the most valuable player."

(8) "There's no mistake," Coach Travis said. "You had 26 points, 11 rebounds, and 8 assists. I'd say that makes you a very valuable player."

(9) "But I missed that last shot," Scott said. "We lost the game because of me."

(10) "I don't know about that," said Coach Travis. "Everybody misses a shot from time to time. Don't be so hard on yourself. It's all about perspective."

(11) "What do you mean?" Scott asked.

(12) "Well," Coach Travis answered, "you could say you are the reason we lost the game because you missed that last shot. On the other hand, you could say you are the reason we almost won because of your awesome performance throughout the game. How you look at it is up to you."

(13) Scott's teammates came running over and surrounded Coach Travis. They jostled one another playfully, talking and laughing.

(14) "Hey, Coach," one player called out, "how about treating your team to pizza?"

(15) "I don't know," said Coach Travis. "Do you think you deserve pizza?"

(16) Scott piped up. "Of course we do! After all, we almost won the game."

(17) Coach Travis smiled. "You're right, Scott. We did almost win. Okay. Pizza for everyone!"

Questions 22-24 pertain to "The Talent Show" short story:

22. Which of the following is the best definition of "forlornly" as it is used in paragraph 5?

a. With a happy spirit
b. With a sad spirit
c. With a lonely spirit
d. With an angry spirit

23. What is the main theme of this story?

a. Real friends support you, no matter what
b. It is easy to forget the words of a song
c. Performing in a talent show can be embarrassing
d. Megan feels like a failure

24. What point of view is used to tell this story?

a. First person
b. Second person
c. Third person
d. None of the above

Questions 25-29 pertain to "The Tournament" short story:

25. In paragraph 4, what does "elated" mean?

a. Happy and excited
b. Frustrated and angry
c. Loud and rowdy
d. Pushy and proud

26. In the first sentence of paragraph 4, what type of figurative language is used?

a. Hyperbole
b. Metaphor
c. Personification
d. Simile

27. Which of the following best expresses the theme of this story?

a. The Eagles want to be the state champions
b. There are different ways to look at any situation
c. Winning isn't everything
d. Scott is a very good basketball player

28. Which of the following is the best summary of this story?

a. At the buzzer, Scott misses an important basket because he isn't a very good basketball player
b. Coach Travis feels Scott is the most valuable player in the game because he scored 26 points
c. When Scott misses an important shot, he is disappointed, but Coach Travis shows him there are different ways to look at the situation
d. The Eagles lose the state championship because of Scott, but Coach Travis sees things differently and makes Scott the most valuable player

29. Why is Scott so upset in this story?

a. He feels responsible for losing the game
b. He thinks he is a bad basketball player
c. He doesn't like Coach Travis
d. He doesn't want to play basketball anymore

Questions 30-31 pertain to both "The Talent Show" and "The Tournament" short stories:

30. In what ways are Scott and Megan most similar in these stories?

a. They are both performers.
b. They are both very active.
c. They are both disappointed in themselves.
d. They both have good friends.

31. What general theme is evident in both stories?

a. Winning is important, but it isn't everything
b. Good friends are the most valuable thing in life
c. Coaches can offer good perspective on tough situations
d. When you try your best, you shouldn't be disappointed in yourself

Questions 32-40 pertain to the following story:

Everybody's Problem

(1) I used to think homeless people were dirty and lazy and mean. I thought they were all old men with scraggly beards and mangy dogs. I thought they lived on the street because they wanted to. I thought they were all drug addicts and alcoholics who ate from garbage cans and slept in boxes. I used to think homelessness wasn't my problem. Then I met Chris, and he showed me I was wrong—about everything. Homelessness is everybody's problem.

(2) The sun was climbing into the bright blue sky as we loaded up the bus at the youth center. It was a crisp, cold Thanksgiving morning, and our youth group was headed down to a local shelter called The Lighthouse. We were going to serve Thanksgiving dinner to more than a hundred homeless people. It seemed like an appropriate way to spend Thanksgiving Day.

(3) When we arrived at the shelter, we were each given a job to do. My job was peeling potatoes. The shelter director gave me a peeler and a garbage can and sat me down in front of a giant pile of potatoes. I had never seen so many potatoes in one place before. They rose from the tray like Mt. Everest. By the time I had peeled them all, my hands and arms and shoulders ached.

(4) When the kitchen work was done, we were given our serving stations. The director explained that this was the only meal many of the homeless people would eat that day, and for some, it was the only hot meal they would have that week. Even so, there wasn't a lot of food for so many people. We were supposed to give each person one slice of turkey, one scoop of mashed potatoes, one scoop of stuffing, a small drizzle of gravy, a few green beans, and a sliver of pumpkin pie.

(5) I was plodding along, dishing up mashed potatoes with an ice cream scoop, when I happened to look up at the person I was serving. He wasn't a dirty, bearded old man. He was a boy about my age, with brown hair and brown eyes and a patched green jacket.

(6) "Hi," the boy said. "I'm Chris."

(7) "I'm Ben," I said as I scooped some potatoes onto his plate. "Happy Thanksgiving."

(8) "Thanks," Chris said, and then he was gone.

(9) As Chris moved down the line, I began to look around, really seeing things for the first time. Very few of the homeless people fit my stereotype. There were men and women, old and young. Children played in a corner of the dining room. At one table, teenagers talked in a tight group. People chatted and smiled. A few were even laughing. This was not what I had pictured a homeless shelter would be like.

(10) When everyone had been served, I began to help clean up. I couldn't help watching Chris as I cleared the tables and wiped them down. He was playing peek-a-boo with a little girl in a high chair. I wondered if it was his little sister.

(11) I was so lost in thought that I jumped when the shelter director tapped my shoulder. She laughed.

(12) "I'll finish cleaning up here," she said. "Why don't you go talk to Chris? He's very nice."

(13) As I approached the table where Chris was sitting, I felt nervous. What would I say? Could we possibly have anything to talk about? Would he even want to talk to me? I sat cautiously beside him.

(14) "Hi, Ben," he said.

(15) "Hi, Chris. Is that your little sister?"

(16) Chris smiled. "Yep. This is Sophia. And over there is my little brother, Dane." Chris motioned toward the corner where the smaller children were playing. Then he pointed to a dark-haired woman at a nearby table. "That's my mom."

(17) "Are you all homeless?" I asked.

(18) "Yep," answered Chris. "We've been here at The Lighthouse for almost two months now. It's okay here, but I miss my old school and my friends. I hope we can move back to a real house soon."

(19) "I didn't know there was such a thing as homeless kids," I admitted.

(20) "Me neither," said Chris. "At least, not until I became one."

(21) "How did it happen?" I asked. Then I had second thoughts. "I mean, you don't have to tell me if you don't want to. I was just wondering."

(22) "It's okay," Chris said. "I don't mind talking about it. About a year ago, my dad got really sick. He was in the hospital for a few months. Then he died. We didn't have any insurance or anything, and my mom couldn't get a job. Besides, she was really sad, and she was trying to take care of me and Dane and Sophia."

(23) "So, how did you end up homeless?" I wondered.

(24) "Mom says there were just too many bills and not enough money. First, we got our lights turned off. Then we couldn't pay our rent, so we had to move out of our house. We stayed with friends for a while, but eventually there was nobody left to stay with. So, we came here."

(25) "Will you stay here forever?" I asked.

(26) "No," Chris said. "My mom is in a program to give her training and help her get a job. When she finds a job, we can get a new place to live. Then things can be normal again."

(27) I heard my youth leader calling for us to load the bus. I wanted to talk to Chris more and ask him more questions, but I knew I had to leave. I stood up.

(28) "I have to go," I said. "I'm glad I got to meet you, Chris. I hope you get a new house soon."

(29) "Thanks, Ben," Chris said. "It was nice to meet you, too. Thanks for hanging out with me for a while. Happy Thanksgiving."

(30) "Happy Thanksgiving," I echoed as I headed toward the door. When I looked back, Chris waved. Then he started playing peek-a-boo with Sophia again.

(31) I will probably never see Chris again, but I have thought of him many times since that day. In just a few minutes together, he taught me so much about the problem of homelessness. It isn't just a problem that affects lazy, mean old men. It affects men and women of all ages. It affects children. It affects whole families. It affected Chris. And because I got the chance to see homelessness through his eyes, it affects me now, too. I think I'll go back again next Thanksgiving ... or maybe sooner. After all, now I know that homelessness is everybody's problem.

32. What is the setting for this story?

a. A youth center
b. A homeless shelter
c. A community center
d. A school

33. If you were describing this story, what classification would you use?

a. Memoir
b. Biography
c. Autobiography
d. Fiction

34. In paragraph 9, what does the word "stereotype" mean?

a. A textbook definition of a concept
b. Height, weight, and physical features
c. A generalized idea of what something is like
d. A description given by an authority figure

35. What point of view is used to tell this story?

a. First person
b. Second person
c. Third person
d. All of the above

36. What is the main theme of this story?

a. Kids can be homeless
b. Potatoes are difficult to peel
c. Serving at a homeless shelter is a good Thanksgiving project
d. Homelessness is everybody's problem

37. What does the author compare the potatoes to in paragraph 3?

a. A tower
b. A mountain range
c. Mt. Everest
d. A mound

38. Which of the following items was not included in the Thanksgiving dinner at the shelter?

a. Turkey
b. Cranberry sauce
c. Mashed potatoes and gravy
d. Pumpkin pie

39. What major event in the life of Chris's family led to their homelessness?

a. Their house burned down
b. Chris's mom lost her job
c. They had to live in their car
d. Chris's dad got sick and died

40. How does meeting Chris change Ben's mind about homelessness?

a. It doesn't change Ben's mind at all
b. It makes Ben afraid of being homeless
c. It helps Ben see that homelessness affects everyone
d. It keeps Ben from ever helping in a homeless shelter again

Answer Key and Explanations

1. B: A simile compares one thing to another by using "like" or "as"; the only simile in paragraph 1—"like a mirage"—refers to the path.

2. C: "Landlocked" means "not on a waterway."

3. A: This information is found in Paragraph 5: "In March of 1973, the first Anchorage to Nome Iditarod Trail race was organized and held. This race was much longer than previous races, covering more than 1,000 miles—the whole Iditarod Trail."

4. D: This is an informational article – the author's main purpose in writing this article is to educate the reader about the Iditarod Trail.

5. D: The descriptive word "desperate" and the descriptive phrase "cry for help" are used in reference to the doctors in Nome in 1925.

6. A: Historical overviews, like this one, are best written in the third-person point of view.

7. C: We learn in Paragraph 5 that the Iditarod Trail became a National Historic Trail in 1978.

8. B: This answer offers the most accurate summary of the history of the Iditarod Trail race.

9. A: This article is organized chronologically, from earliest to latest dates.

10. C: is a supporting detail that expands on a main idea from the article. A, B, and D are not the best choices because they are all main points in the article instead of supporting details.

11. B: is We learn in Paragraph 7 that the race participants receive their racing order numbers at the first mushers' banquet.

12. D: We learn in Paragraph 8 that, as they begin the Iditarod Trail race, mushers are separated by two-minute intervals.

13. C: The phrase "ancient history" is a figure of speech. Amy uses it to communicate that she has totally forgotten about the fight.

14. A: Scene 1 is set on the school steps.

15. C: Scene 2 and Scene 3 take place in a cosmetics store.

16. B: Scene 2 contains the climax of the play, when Jessica must decide whether to go along with Amy or not. In a story, the climax is the most exciting part of the story, when the action or tension builds to a zenith. This occurred when Jessica learned that Amy was planning on stealing the lipstick.

17. A: The word "gonna" is used to show Amy's slang speech pattern.

18. D: The use of "ancient history" in paragraph 6 is a hyperbole, a major exaggeration.

19. B: The tone of this play is conversational.

20. B: The underlying theme of the play is that you should always do the right thing, even when it's difficult. This could also be called the moral of the story.

21. C: is the most accurate and complete summary of the play.

22. B: "Forlornly" is best defined as "with a sad spirit."

23. A most accurately represents the main theme of the story.

24. C: This story is written in the third person. That means the author is writing from the point of view of a narrator – someone who knows all the details of the story but isn't involved in it.

25. A: If someone is "elated", they are extremely happy and excited about something.

26. D: The first sentence of paragraph 4 uses a simile when it says Scott "stood like a statue." A simile uses "like" or "as" to compare one thing to another.

27. B most clearly and completely expresses the theme of the story. Coach Travis tells Scott that "it's all about perspective", and then says that how Scott decides to look at it is up to him.

28. C is the most complete and accurate summary of the story overall. A, B, and D are incorrect because they cover only part of the story or some of the main ideas and concepts.

29. A: Scott is upset in the story because he feels responsible for the team's loss.

30. C: Scott and Megan are most similar in their feelings of disappointment in themselves.

31. D: clearly reflects a general theme found in both stories.

32. B: This story is set at a homeless shelter.

33. A: This story is written in the style of a memoir, as evidenced by the first-person, reflective tone.

34. C offers the best definition of "stereotype" as it is used in paragraph 9.

35. A: This story is written in first person. That means the author is involved in the events of the story and is telling it from his point of view.

36. D: The main theme of the story is that homelessness is everybody's problem. One clue that this is the main point of the story is that the author clearly states it in the last line of the story. It's not always true that the last line of a short piece contains the main point, but that is often the case.

37. C: In paragraph 3 the author uses a simile to compare the size of the pile of potatoes to Mt. Everest.

38. B: Cranberry sauce was not served as part of the Thanksgiving dinner at the shelter.

39. D: The death of Chris's dad was the major problem the family had to deal with that eventually led to their homelessness.

40. C: After meeting Chris, Ben had a completely different view of homelessness. Prior to the Thanksgiving meal, Ben thought homeless people were nothing but a bunch of old, filthy drunks and drug addicts. Meeting Ben and his family helped him understand that homelessness can happen to all kinds of people.

Reading Practice Test #2

Questions 1 – 12 pertain to the following article:

THE TROUBLE WITH TESTS

(1) Lisa was a good student. She studied hard, diligently did her homework, and turned in assignments on time. Whenever she had to take a test, however, Lisa had a problem. Her hands began to sweat and her stomach began to churn. She felt dizzy and breathless and sick. As a result, Lisa couldn't focus and always did poorly on tests. Her grades suffered, and so did her confidence level.

(2) Lisa's problem is a common one. Often called test anxiety, it includes any unusual stress symptoms that occur during tests. Symptoms can be as mild as light nausea or headache, or as severe as vomiting or uncontrollable shaking. Millions of students deal with test anxiety every year, but few realize it can be improved through three simple steps.

(3) The first step to improving test anxiety is better study habits. Proper preparation is an important step to overcoming test anxiety. It is important to develop regular study times, avoiding last minute "cramming" for a test. Studying heavily on the day of or night before a test can actually increase test anxiety in most students. The better option is to devote at least a half-hour block of time to reviewing class materials each day. This can help embed information in the brain, making it more accessible at test time.

(4) Using memory games and tools is another way to improve study habits. Using these tools and games can help students better retain information. It also makes learning more fun, reducing stress levels. Flashcards with key points or ideas can be very helpful when used alone or with a study partner. Mnemonic devices—silly sayings to help students recall complex concepts—are also helpful tools for reducing stress and improving test performance. An example of a mnemonic device is "Every Good Boy Deserves Fudge" to help music students remember the note names for the lines of the treble clef staff (EGBDF).

(5) The second step to reducing test anxiety is to use relaxation techniques. The first relaxation technique that is useful for test anxiety is visualization. This involves choosing a favorite place or event. When test anxiety symptoms appear, students can close their eyes and visualize themselves in that favorite place or at that favorite event. The students should focus on sensory information—sights, sounds, smells, etc. This refocuses the attention of the brain and reduces anxiety.

(6) Another relaxation technique that works well for test anxiety is deep breathing. When the body is under stress, breathing becomes shallower, causing the heart rate to increase and the blood pressure to rise. Conscious deep breathing helps increase oxygen flow to the body, reducing the heart rate and blood pressure. To do deep breathing, simply draw air in through the nose for five seconds, and then release the air through the mouth, blowing out steadily for five seconds. Done with eyes open or closed, deep breathing exercises reduce stress and relax the body.

(7) The third step to reducing test anxiety is positive self-talk. Often, test anxiety is the result of or is compounded by a lack of faith in abilities. Students can overcome this through positive self-talk and self-affirmation. Before each test, a student should repeat, "I can do this"—or some similar positive mantra—over and over. This can be done out loud or silently; either way, it creates a positive attitude and outlook that can reduce anxiety.

(8) The self-affirmation of celebrating success is a final key to overcoming test anxiety. Students should share test-taking victories with friends and loved ones. Students should also feel proud when they do well on a test. Every success is a blow to the obstacle of test anxiety. As with anything else, practice makes perfect, and celebrating success helps a student practice triumph over test anxiety.

(9) Test anxiety is a real problem, not an imagined issue or an excuse. It can be overcome, however, through three basic steps. First, students must use study tools and good habits for proper preparation. Second, students must use relaxation techniques—such as visualization and deep breathing—to help release stress from the body. Finally, students must engage in positive self-talk and celebrate successes to create an atmosphere of triumph. When all three of these steps are consistently practiced, test anxiety will become a thing of the past.

1. According to this article, what is test anxiety?

a. A hereditary psychological disease
b. Unusual stress symptoms that occur during tests
c. An allergy to stress that is triggered by tests
d. Headaches and nausea that occur after tests

2. What is a mnemonic device?

a. A silly saying used to help remember a complex concept
b. A tool that increases physical relaxation during a test
c. An old-fashioned torture device involving repeated testing
d. A tool for selecting answers on tests

3. What is the main purpose of this article?

a. To show that test anxiety is a common problem
b. To discuss Lisa's problems with test anxiety
c. To identify the symptoms of test anxiety
d. To identify potential solutions for test anxiety

4. What is the general tone of this article?

a. Entertaining
b. Persuasive
c. Informative
d. Fictional

5. Which of the following offers the best summary of this article?

a. Test anxiety is a common problem that can be improved through three simple steps
b. Lisa has test anxiety, and she needs to learn how to deal with it better
c. Relaxation techniques are the best method for preventing test anxiety
d. Good study habits are the best tools for preventing test anxiety

6. According to paragraph 3, what common study practice should be avoided?

a. Using flashcards
b. Studying with a partner
c. Last-minute studying
d. Overstudying

7. What is the first step to improving test anxiety?

a. Better study habits
b. Relaxation techniques
c. Self-affirmation and positive self-talk
d. Teamwork and study partners

8. What is the third step to reducing test anxiety?

a. Better study habits
b. Positive self-talk
c. Visualization
d. Relaxation techniques

9. Which of the following ideas is a supporting detail in this article?

a. Millions of students deal with test anxiety every year
b. Using memory games and tools improves study habits
c. Test anxiety is a real problem
d. "Every Good Boy Deserves Fudge" is an example of a study tool

10. What organizational pattern is used for this article?

a. Inverted pyramid
b. Proposition and support
c. Problem and solution
d. Simple exposition

11. What two specific relaxation techniques are discussed in this article?

a. Massage and deep breathing
b. Visualization and muscle tensing
c. Meditation and massage
d. Visualization and deep breathing

12. Which paragraph discusses the "final key" to overcoming test anxiety?

a. Paragraph 6
b. Paragraph 8
c. Paragraph 7
d. Paragraph 9

Questions 13-17 pertain to the following poem:

Fog

(1) Stealthy fog drifts through the air,
(2) A dense, gray blanket everywhere.
(3) It slowly seeps in from the sea,
(4) Clutching rooftops, climbing trees.

(5) Its eerie whisper fills the land—
(6) "Catch me, catch me, if you can!"
(7) It skims the sky and hugs the ground,
(8) Distorts the vision, muffles sound.

(9) It fills the mind and fools the feet
(10) Like haunting shadows in the street.
(11) It creeps across the alleyway
(12) And dims the newborn light of day.

(13) It smothers landscapes without shame
(14) Then fades as quickly as it came.

13. Which of the following is the best synonym for "stealthy"?

a. Evil
b. Careful
c. Sneaky
d. Thick

14. What type of figurative language is used in line 5?

a. Personification
b. Metaphor
c. Simile
d. Hyperbole

15. What does the poet accomplish by using figurative language throughout this poem?

a. The poet meets the basic requirements of poetry
b. The poet makes the fog seem alive
c. The poet confuses and overwhelms the reader
d. The poet gives additional length to the poem

16. To what is the fog compared in line 2?

a. A whisper
b. The sea
c. A shadow
d. A blanket

17. Which of the following best describes the rhyming pattern of this poem?

a. ABAB CDCD EFEF GG
b. AAAA BBBB CCCC DD
c. ABCD EFGH IJKL MN
d. AABB CCDD EEFF GG

Questions 18 – 20 pertain to the following poem:

Summer Afternoon

(1) Golden sunlight bathes the meadow

(2) In brilliant midday glory.

(3) Slim green pillars bow in homage

(4) To a gentle summer breeze.

(5) Flowers turn their eager faces

(6) Upward to an azure sky.

(7) All is quiet, calm, and peaceful,

(8) Dozing in the pleasant heat.

(9) Just across the sleepy meadow

(10) A lazy stream meanders through,

(11) Sauntering between the banks

(12) Of hardened, sun-baked earth.

(13) Dragonflies flit to and fro

(14) Like scattered thoughts and fleeting dreams.

(15) Bright light glistens on the water

(16) Like sparkling, molten silver.

(17) The meadow rests in tacit glow

(18) As minutes turn to hours.

(19) The sun sinks lower in the sky,

(20) And shadows slowly lengthen.

(21) Daylight, dappled by the trees,

(22) Spreads across the open landscape

(23) Like a dim and dusky cloak,

(24) And—in silence—evening falls.

18. What do lines 3 and 4 refer to in a metaphor?

a. Green buildings in the field
b. Grasses waving in the wind
c. Trees waving in the wind
d. People worshipping the wind

19. What does "tacit" mean in line 17?

a. Beautiful
b. Lazy
c. Silent
d. Bored

20. Which of the following best describes the mood of this poem?

a. Upbeat and exciting
b. Quiet and peaceful
c. Depressing and sullen
d. Happy and energetic

Questions 21 -22 pertain to both "Fog" and "Summer Afternoon":

21. What general theme is represented in both of these poems?

a. Nature
b. Water
c. Emotions
d. Time

22. What is the most important difference in the style of these two poems?

a. One uses figurative language and the other does not
b. One is longer than the other
c. One is set at night and the other is set in the daytime
d. One is rhymed and the other is free verse

Questions 23 – 32 pertain to the following story:

The Memory Quilt

(1) Kevin had been saving his allowance for months to buy a new bike. Now he was within a few dollars of his goal, and Grandma Ruth had offered to pay him to clean out her attic. Kevin was excited. The new bike was practically his!

(2) Early Saturday morning, Kevin's mom dropped him off at Grandma Ruth's house. Grandma Ruth hugged him. Then she walked upstairs with him and pointed him to a narrow ladder that led up to the attic.

(3) "It's a mess up there," she warned. "If you have any questions about anything, just ask. Most of it is old junk, though. You can sort things I won't want to keep into two piles—one to throw away and the other to donate to charity."

(4) Kevin climbed the ladder and looked around. Boxes and piles of old pictures and records and clothes littered the floor. It was a big job. He picked up a painting of flowers in a chipped wooden frame. It didn't look important, but Kevin thought he should check.

(5) "Grandma Ruth," he called, climbing down the ladder with the picture. "Is this important?"

(6) Grandma Ruth came out of her room and chuckled. "No, Kevin. Your grandfather and I bought that old picture at a yard sale years ago. Put it in the pile to donate to charity."

(7) Kevin climbed back up the ladder. He put the picture on the floor to start a pile for charity. Then he picked up an old, rusty toolbox. Like the old picture, it didn't look important, but Kevin thought he should check, just to make sure.

(8) "Grandma Ruth," he called again, climbing down the ladder with the toolbox. "Is this important?"

(9) Grandma Ruth laughed gently. "No, Kevin. Your grandfather bought that toolbox when we bought this old house. He was quite the handyman. But I have no use for it now. Put it in the pile to donate. And Kevin?"

(10) "Yes, Grandma Ruth?"

(11) "You don't have to check with me about each thing. If it looks old and unused, you can donate it or throw it away. I trust your judgment. But you can still ask if you have any questions." She winked at Kevin and went back into her room.

(12) Kevin climbed back up the ladder. He sorted through the piles quickly. By lunchtime, he was almost halfway done. He climbed down and ate tuna fish sandwiches with Grandma Ruth in the dining room. After lunch, she gave him some boxes to take up to the attic. She told him to box up and carry down the items to be donated to charity.

(13) Kevin made his way awkwardly back to the attic, carrying the boxes. He packed things up and sorted through piles until just before 4 pm, when his mom was

coming to pick him up. The last item he grabbed was a faded, dusty quilt. He turned it over and studied it carefully. It was worn, and it seemed like it hadn't been used in a long time. Kevin threw it into a charity box and closed the top. Then he began carrying boxes down the ladder.

(14) Kevin's mom drove him by the Goodwill store on the way home. Together they unloaded the boxes of items to be donated. Then they headed home, where Kevin fell asleep right after dinner. He was exhausted from his hard work.

(15) Sunday afternoon, Kevin went back to Grandma Ruth's house to finish cleaning out the attic. The piles were sparser now, but they still popped up from the dusty floor like wayward molehills. He got right to work, sorting, boxing things up, and neatly stacking the items to be kept.

(16) Halfway through the afternoon, Grandma Ruth called Kevin down for cookies and milk.

(17) "Kevin, have you seen my old patchwork quilt up in the attic?" Grandma Ruth asked. "I can't seem to find it anywhere. I made that quilt from your grandfather's old work shirts and your mom's first baby blanket and the tablecloth I got at my wedding. There are so many memories in that quilt."

(18) Kevin gulped. He didn't want to lie to Grandma Ruth, but he couldn't tell her he donated her precious quilt to charity. She would kill him!

(19) "I'll look for it when I go back up," he promised, knowing it wasn't there.

(20) At the end of the afternoon, Kevin was done cleaning the attic. He carried the last box down the ladder.

(21) "Did you see my quilt up there?" Grandma Ruth asked.

(22) "No," Kevin said, half-truthfully.

(23) "I wonder where it could be," Grandma Ruth said.

(24) When Kevin and his mom stopped at the Goodwill store to donate the last set of boxes, Kevin asked if he could run inside. He dashed in and browsed the shelves carefully. Then he saw it. It was stuffed between two stacks of throw pillows. It was almost hidden, but unmistakable. He pulled out the quilt and checked the price.

(25) Kevin's heart fell. Paying for the quilt would mean he would have to wait another month or two to buy his bike. If he just went home, no one would ever know about his mistake. But he knew that would be wrong. Buying the quilt back was the right thing to do. Kevin paid for the quilt and hurried back to the car.

(26) Kevin's mom looked at the quilt with surprise. "Isn't that Grandma Ruth's memory quilt?"

(27) Kevin nodded glumly. He told his mom the whole story. Then he said he needed to go back to Grandma Ruth's house to tell her the truth.

(28) "I'm proud of you," Kevin's mom said as she turned the car around. "Let's go give Grandma Ruth back her memories."

23. Which of the following is the best definition of "littered" as it is used in paragraph 4?

a. Stacked neatly on
b. Scattered across
c. Piled on
d. Put in a few places

24. What is the primary setting for this story?

a. Grandma Ruth's attic
b. The Goodwill store
c. Kevin's house
d. Grandma Ruth's dining room

25. In paragraph 15, what does "sparser" mean?

a. Denser
b. Larger and higher
c. Fewer and smaller
d. More organized

26. What is the general theme of this story?

a. Help your grandmother
b. Cleaning is best done in an organized way
c. Do the right thing
d. Never throw away or donate old items

27. Which paragraph contains the climax of this story?

a. Paragraph 12
b. Paragraph 16
c. Paragraph 24
d. Paragraph 25

28. Why was the quilt so valuable to Grandma Ruth?

a. It contained fabric from memorable things
b. It was sewn by hand by her grandmother
c. She had used the quilt for many years
d. It was a wedding present from Kevin's grandfather

29. Which of the following is a supporting detail in this story?

a. Kevin was saving his allowance for a new bike
b. Kevin and Grandma Ruth ate tuna fish sandwiches
c. Kevin was cleaning out Grandma Ruth's attic
d. Kevin donated Grandma Ruth's quilt to charity

30. Which of the following is the best summary of this story?

a. Kevin spends his Saturday cleaning out Grandma Ruth's attic so he can buy a bike
b. While cleaning out Grandma Ruth's attic, Kevin donates an important quilt to charity and has to get it back
c. Grandma Ruth describes her memory quilt to Kevin while eating cookies and milk
d. Kevin and his mom take Grandma Ruth's memory quilt back to her after finding it and buying it at Goodwill

31. Which of the following elements was not part of the memory quilt?

a. Grandma Ruth's wedding dress
b. Grandfather's old work shirts
c. Kevin's mom's baby blanket
d. Grandma Ruth's tablecloth

32. What type of figurative language is used at the end of paragraph 18?

a. Simile
b. Metaphor
c. Personification
d. Hyperbole

Questions 33 – 40 pertain to the following article:

LIKE RIDING A KITE

(1) Imagine soaring high above the earth. There is no engine, no fuselage beneath you. There is only you, your glider, the wind, and the sky. It's like riding a kite with no strings attached, rising and falling on the breeze like a bird. It is freedom and thrill and ultimate pleasure. This is the world of hang gliding.

(2) While many people have a general idea of what hang gliding is all about, few really understand the sport. Most people don't realize a majestic glider can be collapsed to the size of a duffel bag. Few people know that gliders can stay aloft for hours and that the world distance record for a single glider flight is nearly 190 miles. Even fewer people realize that a hang glider can actually climb in the sky, even without an engine. In California, in the 1980s, one expert glider pilot gained more than 14,000 feet of altitude after takeoff! Hang gliders have mind-boggling capabilities.

(3) The amazing sport of hang gliding has a rich history dating back to the 1890s. In 1891, the first hang glider was invented by Otto Lilienthal in Germany. It was made of wood and cloth, weighed 40 pounds, was 23 feet wide, and could go about 35 miles per hour (mph) at an altitude of 100 feet. British inventor Percy Picher also built gliders with similar features in the late 1890s. Unfortunately, both inventors were killed in glider crashes before their designs were perfected. With the element of danger involved in early hang gliding—and with the advent of airplane flight by the Wright brothers in 1903—many people lost interest in hang gliding.

(4) After the end of World War II, however, many military-trained pilots wanted to keep flying. Airplanes were too expensive for most people, so the sport of hang gliding was reborn. Through invention and innovation, new designs for hang gliders began to emerge. These included new materials and designs for glider construction

and the addition of a control bar to improve safety. The basic design for today's hang gliders premiered at a meet in California in 1971. It included a broad, flexible wing on a sturdy frame with a control bar and a seat or safety harness.

(5) Since 1971, few major design changes have been made to hang gliders, although as new materials for construction become available, minor changes are made to improve flight. Modern sails range from 13 to 28 feet across. They are made of durable, lightweight, manmade fabric—such as nylon—and are designed to flex in shape and tension based on the wind. The sail is attached to a frame made from aluminum tubing. The frame includes a control bar, shaped like a rounded triangle and used for steering. Suspended from the frame is a harness or seat to improve pilot comfort and safety.

(6) Another way pilots improve comfort and safety is through the use of proper gear and equipment. Pilots should wear light, protective clothing and gloves designed for hang gliding. A helmet is also an important safety component. In addition, pilots need special instruments that are used during flight. These tools help measure thermals, the warm air currents used to lift and propel gliders through the air.

(7) Thermals are important to both taking off and staying aloft, but they aren't the only factor in flight. Modern gliders weigh about 35 pounds and are special balanced to a pilot's weight and preferences. To take off, the pilot is secured in the glider and then runs off the edge of a large hill or cliff, where thermals catch the glider and lift it into the air. If the wind is sustained at 12 mph or above, the pilot may even be able to take off without running. Once the glider is airborne, the pilot steers by shifting his/her weight and using the control bar. Each glider has its own unique feel, and a pilot must know the glider well to achieve a safe takeoff, flight, and landing.

(8) In addition to knowing the unique feel of the glider, a pilot must know the safety rules of the sky to have a safe flight. Pilots of hang gliders do not need to be licensed, but they must obey all rules and laws for flying. Hang glider pilots should never fly in bad weather or high winds. They must yield the right of way to any aircraft in distress and all hot air balloons. They must never intentionally fly into a cloud or a flock of birds. Finally, hang glider pilots should stay at least five miles away from airports during flight and at least 100 feet from buildings, telephone wires and poles, populated places, and crowds.

(9) Throughout history, mankind has looked for a way to soar with the birds across the canvas of the sky. Hang gliding offers that opportunity. With modern features and equipment, and with proper training in techniques and the rules of the sky, hang glider pilots can safely experience the thrill of flight. In a glider, the pilot is one with the breeze, the sunlight, the world itself. Hang gliding is truly like riding a kite through the expanse of the heavens.

33. In paragraph 3, what does "advent" mean?

a. End
b. Beginning
c. Expansion
d. Popularity

34. What was the author's main purpose in writing this article?

a. To inform
b. To entertain
c. To analyze
d. To persuade

35. From what point of view is this article written?

a. First person
b. Second person
c. Third person
d. All of the above

36. Which of the following best describes the theme of this article?

a. Hang gliding has a rich history that began in the 1890s with two inventors
b. Modern hang gliding has come far and is a safe, fun way to soar through the sky
c. Hang gliders are 13 to 28 feet wide and have a sturdy frame and harness or seat
d. The modern hang glider premiered at a meet in California in 1971

37. What material is used to make modern hang glider frames?

a. Aluminum
b. Steel
c. Wood
d. PVC

38. Which of the following is a main idea in this article?

a. Modern glider sails are 13 to 28 feet wide
b. Glider pilots must know the rules of the sky
c. All glider pilots should wear helmets for safety
d. Modern glider design premiered in 1971

39. How did World War II positively impact the sport of hang gliding?

a. It did not positively impact the sport of hang gliding
b. Gliders were used in World War II in Europe and Asia
c. Returning military pilots wanted to fly but couldn't afford planes
d. Flight had become much safer due to World War II technology

40. How far away from airports should hang glider pilots stay while flying?

a. 100 feet
b. 500 feet
c. 1 mile
d. 5 miles

Answer Key and Explanations

1. B: In paragraph 1, we learn that Lisa does poorly on tests because she suffers from a variety of unusual symptoms whenever she takes a test. In paragraph 2, the author tells us that there's a name for this condition, which is test anxiety.

2. A: The explanation of a mnemonic device is found in paragraph 4.

3. D: The main purpose of this article is to identify potential solutions for test anxiety. The passage starts out by describing what test anxiety is, and then goes on to explain three ways to overcome it.

4. C: The tone of this article is informative. It's not fictional, and it's not trying to entertain readers, or persuade them to do something. It simply gives people information about what test anxiety is, and what they can do about it if they suffer from it.

5. A: This answer choice offers the best summary of the article.

6. C: According to paragraph 3, last-minute studying should be avoided.

7. A: We learn in paragraph 3 that the first step to reducing test anxiety is better study habits.

8. B: Paragraph 7 says the third step to reducing test anxiety is positive self-talk.

9. D: This is the only answer choice that is a supporting detail. In other words, it represents a minor point of the article. A, B, and C are incorrect because they all represent main ideas in the article, not supporting details.

10. C: This article is organized in a problem-and-solution format.

11. D: Two specific relaxation techniques mentioned in the article are visualization and deep breathing. They can be found in paragraphs 5 and 6.

12. B: Paragraph 8 discusses the "final key" to overcoming test anxiety.

13. C: The word *sneaky* has almost the same meaning as *stealthy*, which means "quietly and secretly." When someone is doing something stealthily, they are trying to do something without been seen or heard.

14. A: Personification is using language that attributes human characteristics to non-human things. Line 5 uses personification when it suggests that the fog has an "eerie whisper."

15. B: The poet has filled this poem with figurative language to give the reader the impression that the fog is a living, breathing, thinking creature.

16. D: In line 2, the fog is compared to a "dense, gray blanket."

17. D: The rhyming pattern of this poem is AABB CCDD EEFF GG.

18. B: The metaphor in lines 3 and 4 refers to grasses waving in the wind.

19. C: In line 17, "tacit" means silent.

20. B: The mood of this poem is quiet and peaceful. The author creates this mood by carefully choosing words, phrases, and rhythms to bring about these feelings in the reader.

21. A: Even though the poems are about two different subjects, fog and a summer afternoon, the general theme of both poems is nature.

22. D: The most important difference between the styles of these two poems is that one is rhymed and the other is free verse.

23. B: This is the correct answer because "scattered across" is the best definition of "littered" as it is used in paragraph 4. The author is trying to communicate that in Kevin's mind, junk was "all over the floor."

24. A: Some scenes take place in other places, but the main setting for this story is Grandma Ruth's attic, because that's where the bulk of the story actually takes place.

25. C: The phrase "fewer and smaller" is a good definition for "sparser" as it is used in paragraph 15. Kevin could see that he was making progress because there were fewer piles of junk left, and the ones that remained were smaller than they had been.

26. C: The general theme of this story is "do the right thing." Even though it will cost Kevin some money, and it will mean that he will have to go without a new bike for several more weeks, he goes back to the store and purchases the quilt that meant so much to his grandmother.

27. D: Paragraph 25 contains the climax of the story, when Kevin faces a moral dilemma, and must decide whether he will use his money for the quilt or save it for his bike.

28. A: In paragraph 17, Grandma Ruth tells Kevin that the quilt held so many important memories for her.

29. B: This answer choice is the only one that is a supporting detail. The fact that they had tuna sandwiches for lunch doesn't mean much to the overall story. The other answer choices represent things that are important to the development of the story.

30. B: This is the most clear and accurate summary of the story.

31. A: Grandma Ruth's memory quilt did not include pieces from her wedding dress. The other three answer choices are all elements that were part of Grandma Ruth's memory quilt. This information is found in paragraph 17.

32. D: Hyperbole is exaggeration. Kevin knew that his grandmother would be very upset if she found out that he had thrown out the quilt, but he also knew that there was no way she was going to actually kill him. That was hyperbole.

33. B: The word *advent* means "beginning."

34. A: The author's main purpose in writing this article is to tell the reader about hang gliding – how long it's been taking place, how it got started, how it works, some rules and safety guidelines, etc.

35. C: This article is written in third-person point of view. If the author were talking about his own experiences, using words such as *I* and *me*, then it would be in the first-person.

36. B: is the best choice because it offers the most accurate description of the theme of the article. A, C, and D are all points mentioned in the passage, but they do not accurately and completely describe the theme of the article.

37. A: Modern hang glider frames are made from aluminum. This information can be found in paragraph 5.

38. B: This is the only option that represents a main idea of the article. A, C, and D are not the best choices because they are all supporting details, not main ideas of the article.

39. C: Paragraph 4 says that hang gliding experienced a revival of interest after World War II, when many military pilots were frustrated after coming home from the war, because they couldn't afford to fly planes, so they took up hang gliding.

40. D: Paragraph 8 says hang glider pilots should stay five miles away from airports while flying.

How to Overcome Test Anxiety

Just the thought of taking a test is enough to make most people a little nervous. A test is an important event that can have a long-term impact on your future, so it's important to take it seriously and it's natural to feel anxious about performing well. But just because anxiety is normal, that doesn't mean that it's helpful in test taking, or that you should simply accept it as part of your life. Anxiety can have a variety of effects. These effects can be mild, like making you feel slightly nervous, or severe, like blocking your ability to focus or remember even a simple detail.

If you experience test anxiety—whether severe or mild—it's important to know how to beat it. To discover this, first you need to understand what causes test anxiety.

Causes of Test Anxiety

While we often think of anxiety as an uncontrollable emotional state, it can actually be caused by simple, practical things. One of the most common causes of test anxiety is that a person does not feel adequately prepared for their test. This feeling can be the result of many different issues such as poor study habits or lack of organization, but the most common culprit is time management. Starting to study too late, failing to organize your study time to cover all of the material, or being distracted while you study will mean that you're not well prepared for the test. This may lead to cramming the night before, which will cause you to be physically and mentally exhausted for the test. Poor time management also contributes to feelings of stress, fear, and hopelessness as you realize you are not well prepared but don't know what to do about it.

Other times, test anxiety is not related to your preparation for the test but comes from unresolved fear. This may be a past failure on a test, or poor performance on tests in general. It may come from comparing yourself to others who seem to be performing better or from the stress of living up to expectations. Anxiety may be driven by fears of the future—how failure on this test would affect your educational and career goals. These fears are often completely irrational, but they can still negatively impact your test performance.

Elements of Test Anxiety

As mentioned earlier, test anxiety is considered to be an emotional state, but it has physical and mental components as well. Sometimes you may not even realize that you are suffering from test anxiety until you notice the physical symptoms. These can include trembling hands, rapid heartbeat, sweating, nausea, and tense muscles. Extreme anxiety may lead to fainting or vomiting. Obviously, any of these symptoms can have a negative impact on testing. It is important to recognize them as soon as they begin to occur so that you can address the problem before it damages your performance.

The mental components of test anxiety include trouble focusing and inability to remember learned information. During a test, your mind is on high alert, which can help you recall information and stay focused for an extended period of time. However, anxiety interferes with your mind's natural processes, causing you to blank out, even on the questions you know well. The strain of testing during anxiety makes it difficult to stay focused, especially on a test that may take several hours. Extreme anxiety can take a huge mental toll, making it difficult not only to recall test information but even to understand the test questions or pull your thoughts together.

Effects of Test Anxiety

Test anxiety is like a disease—if left untreated, it will get progressively worse. Anxiety leads to poor performance, and this reinforces the feelings of fear and failure, which in turn lead to poor performances on subsequent tests. It can grow from a mild nervousness to a crippling condition. If allowed to progress, test anxiety can have a big impact on your schooling, and consequently on your future.

Test anxiety can spread to other parts of your life. Anxiety on tests can become anxiety in any stressful situation, and blanking on a test can turn into panicking in a job situation. But fortunately, you don't have to let anxiety rule your testing and determine your grades. There are a number of relatively simple steps you can take to move past anxiety and function normally on a test and in the rest of life.

Physical Steps for Beating Test Anxiety

While test anxiety is a serious problem, the good news is that it can be overcome. It doesn't have to control your ability to think and remember information. While it may take time, you can begin taking steps today to beat anxiety.

Just as your first hint that you may be struggling with anxiety comes from the physical symptoms, the first step to treating it is also physical. Rest is crucial for having a clear, strong mind. If you are tired, it is much easier to give in to anxiety. But if you establish good sleep habits, your body and mind will be ready to perform optimally, without the strain of exhaustion. Additionally, sleeping well helps you to retain information better, so you're more likely to recall the answers when you see the test questions.

Getting good sleep means more than going to bed on time. It's important to allow your brain time to relax. Take study breaks from time to time so it doesn't get overworked, and don't study right before bed. Take time to rest your mind before trying to rest your body, or you may find it difficult to fall asleep.

Along with sleep, other aspects of physical health are important in preparing for a test. Good nutrition is vital for good brain function. Sugary foods and drinks may give a burst of energy but this burst is followed by a crash, both physically and emotionally. Instead, fuel your body with protein and vitamin-rich foods.

Also, drink plenty of water. Dehydration can lead to headaches and exhaustion, especially if your brain is already under stress from the rigors of the test. Particularly if your test is a long one, drink water during the breaks. And if possible, take an energy-boosting snack to eat between sections.

Along with sleep and diet, a third important part of physical health is exercise. Maintaining a steady workout schedule is helpful, but even taking 5-minute study breaks to walk can help get your blood pumping faster and clear your head. Exercise also releases endorphins, which contribute to a positive feeling and can help combat test anxiety.

When you nurture your physical health, you are also contributing to your mental health. If your body is healthy, your mind is much more likely to be healthy as well. So take time to rest, nourish your body with healthy food and water, and get moving as much as possible. Taking these physical steps will make you stronger and more able to take the mental steps necessary to overcome test anxiety.

Mental Steps for Beating Test Anxiety

Working on the mental side of test anxiety can be more challenging, but as with the physical side, there are clear steps you can take to overcome it. As mentioned earlier, test anxiety often stems from lack of preparation, so the obvious solution is to prepare for the test. Effective studying may be the most important weapon you have for beating test anxiety, but you can and should employ several other mental tools to combat fear.

First, boost your confidence by reminding yourself of past success—tests or projects that you aced. If you're putting as much effort into preparing for this test as you did for those, there's no reason you should expect to fail here. Work hard to prepare; then trust your preparation.

Second, surround yourself with encouraging people. It can be helpful to find a study group, but be sure that the people you're around will encourage a positive attitude. If you spend time with others who are anxious or cynical, this will only contribute to your own anxiety. Look for others who are motivated to study hard from a desire to succeed, not from a fear of failure.

Third, reward yourself. A test is physically and mentally tiring, even without anxiety, and it can be helpful to have something to look forward to. Plan an activity following the test, regardless of the outcome, such as going to a movie or getting ice cream.

When you are taking the test, if you find yourself beginning to feel anxious, remind yourself that you know the material. Visualize successfully completing the test. Then take a few deep, relaxing breaths and return to it. Work through the questions carefully but with confidence, knowing that you are capable of succeeding.

Developing a healthy mental approach to test taking will also aid in other areas of life. Test anxiety affects more than just the actual test—it can be damaging to your mental health and even contribute to depression. It's important to beat test anxiety before it becomes a problem for more than testing.

Study Strategy

Being prepared for the test is necessary to combat anxiety, but what does being prepared look like? You may study for hours on end and still not feel prepared. What you need is a strategy for test prep. The next few pages outline our recommended steps to help you plan out and conquer the challenge of preparation.

Step 1: Scope Out the Test

Learn everything you can about the format (multiple choice, essay, etc.) and what will be on the test. Gather any study materials, course outlines, or sample exams that may be available. Not only will this help you to prepare, but knowing what to expect can help to alleviate test anxiety.

Step 2: Map Out the Material

Look through the textbook or study guide and make note of how many chapters or sections it has. Then divide these over the time you have. For example, if a book has 15 chapters and you have five days to study, you need to cover three chapters each day. Even better, if you have the time, leave an extra day at the end for overall review after you have gone through the material in depth.

If time is limited, you may need to prioritize the material. Look through it and make note of which sections you think you already have a good grasp on, and which need review. While you are studying, skim quickly through the familiar sections and take more time on the challenging parts.

Write out your plan so you don't get lost as you go. Having a written plan also helps you feel more in control of the study, so anxiety is less likely to arise from feeling overwhelmed at the amount to cover.

Step 3: Gather Your Tools

Decide what study method works best for you. Do you prefer to highlight in the book as you study and then go back over the highlighted portions? Or do you type out notes of the important information? Or is it helpful to make flashcards that you can carry with you? Assemble the pens, index cards, highlighters, post-it notes, and any other materials you may need so you won't be distracted by getting up to find things while you study.

If you're having a hard time retaining the information or organizing your notes, experiment with different methods. For example, try color-coding by subject with colored pens, highlighters, or post-it notes. If you learn better by hearing, try recording yourself reading your notes so you can listen while in the car, working out, or simply sitting at your desk. Ask a friend to quiz you from your flashcards, or try teaching someone the material to solidify it in your mind.

Step 4: Create Your Environment

It's important to avoid distractions while you study. This includes both the obvious distractions like visitors and the subtle distractions like an uncomfortable chair (or a too-comfortable couch that makes you want to fall asleep). Set up the best study environment possible: good lighting and a comfortable work area. If background music helps you focus, you may want to turn it on, but otherwise keep the room quiet. If you are using a computer to take notes, be sure you don't have any other windows open, especially applications like social media, games, or anything else that could distract you. Silence your phone and turn off notifications. Be sure to keep water close by so you stay hydrated while you study (but avoid unhealthy drinks and snacks).

Also, take into account the best time of day to study. Are you freshest first thing in the morning? Try to set aside some time then to work through the material. Is your mind clearer in the afternoon or evening? Schedule your study session then. Another method is to study at the same time of day that you will take the test, so that your brain gets used to working on the material at that time and will be ready to focus at test time.

Step 5: Study!

Once you have done all the study preparation, it's time to settle into the actual studying. Sit down, take a few moments to settle your mind so you can focus, and begin to follow your study plan. Don't give in to distractions or let yourself procrastinate. This is your time to prepare so you'll be ready to fearlessly approach the test. Make the most of the time and stay focused.

Of course, you don't want to burn out. If you study too long you may find that you're not retaining the information very well. Take regular study breaks. For example, taking five minutes out of every hour to walk briskly, breathing deeply and swinging your arms, can help your mind stay fresh.

As you get to the end of each chapter or section, it's a good idea to do a quick review. Remind yourself of what you learned and work on any difficult parts. When you feel that you've mastered the material, move on to the next part. At the end of your study session, briefly skim through your notes again.

But while review is helpful, cramming last minute is NOT. If at all possible, work ahead so that you won't need to fit all your study into the last day. Cramming overloads your brain with more information than it can process and retain, and your tired mind may struggle to recall even previously learned information when it is overwhelmed with last-minute study. Also, the urgent nature of cramming and the stress placed on your brain contribute to anxiety. You'll be more likely to go to the test feeling unprepared and having trouble thinking clearly.

So don't cram, and don't stay up late before the test, even just to review your notes at a leisurely pace. Your brain needs rest more than it needs to go over the information again. In fact, plan to finish your studies by noon or early afternoon the day before the test. Give your brain the rest of the day to relax or focus on other things, and get a good night's sleep. Then you will be fresh for the test and better able to recall what you've studied.

Step 6: Take a Practice Test

Many courses offer sample tests, either online or in the study materials. This is an excellent resource to check whether you have mastered the material, as well as to prepare for the test format and environment.

Check the test format ahead of time: the number of questions, the type (multiple choice, free response, etc.), and the time limit. Then create a plan for working through them. For example, if you have 30 minutes to take a 60-question test, your limit is 30 seconds per question. Spend less time on the questions you know well so that you can take more time on the difficult ones.

If you have time to take several practice tests, take the first one open book, with no time limit. Work through the questions at your own pace and make sure you fully understand them. Gradually work up to taking a test under test conditions: sit at a desk with all study materials put away and set a timer. Pace yourself to make sure you finish the test with time to spare and go back to check your answers if you have time.

After each test, check your answers. On the questions you missed, be sure you understand why you missed them. Did you misread the question (tests can use tricky wording)? Did you forget the information? Or was it something you hadn't learned? Go back and study any shaky areas that the practice tests reveal.

Taking these tests not only helps with your grade, but also aids in combating test anxiety. If you're already used to the test conditions, you're less likely to worry about it, and working through tests until you're scoring well gives you a confidence boost. Go through the practice tests until you feel comfortable, and then you can go into the test knowing that you're ready for it.

Test Tips

On test day, you should be confident, knowing that you've prepared well and are ready to answer the questions. But aside from preparation, there are several test day strategies you can employ to maximize your performance.

First, as stated before, get a good night's sleep the night before the test (and for several nights before that, if possible). Go into the test with a fresh, alert mind rather than staying up late to study.

Try not to change too much about your normal routine on the day of the test. It's important to eat a nutritious breakfast, but if you normally don't eat breakfast at all, consider eating just a protein bar. If you're a coffee drinker, go ahead and have your normal coffee. Just make sure you time it so that the caffeine doesn't wear off right in the middle of your test. Avoid sugary beverages, and drink enough water to stay hydrated but not so much that you need a restroom break 10 minutes into the test. If your test isn't first thing in the morning, consider going for a walk or doing a light workout before the test to get your blood flowing.

Allow yourself enough time to get ready, and leave for the test with plenty of time to spare so you won't have the anxiety of scrambling to arrive in time. Another reason to be early is to select a good seat. It's helpful to sit away from doors and windows, which can be distracting. Find a good seat, get out your supplies, and settle your mind before the test begins.

When the test begins, start by going over the instructions carefully, even if you already know what to expect. Make sure you avoid any careless mistakes by following the directions.

Then begin working through the questions, pacing yourself as you've practiced. If you're not sure on an answer, don't spend too much time on it, and don't let it shake your confidence. Either skip it and come back later, or eliminate as many wrong answers as possible and guess among the remaining ones. Don't dwell on these questions as you continue—put them out of your mind and focus on what lies ahead.

Be sure to read all of the answer choices, even if you're sure the first one is the right answer. Sometimes you'll find a better one if you keep reading. But don't second-guess yourself if you do immediately know the answer. Your gut instinct is usually right. Don't let test anxiety rob you of the information you know.

If you have time at the end of the test (and if the test format allows), go back and review your answers. Be cautious about changing any, since your first instinct tends to be correct, but make sure you didn't misread any of the questions or accidentally mark the wrong answer choice. Look over any you skipped and make an educated guess.

At the end, leave the test feeling confident. You've done your best, so don't waste time worrying about your performance or wishing you could change anything. Instead, celebrate the successful completion of this test. And finally, use this test to learn how to deal with anxiety even better next time.

Review Video: Test Anxiety
Visit mometrix.com/academy and enter code: 100340

Important Qualification

Not all anxiety is created equal. If your test anxiety is causing major issues in your life beyond the classroom or testing center, or if you are experiencing troubling physical symptoms related to your anxiety, it may be a sign of a serious physiological or psychological condition. If this sounds like your situation, we strongly encourage you to seek professional help.

Online Resources

Due to our efforts to try to keep this book to a manageable length, we've created a link that will give you access to all of your online resources:

mometrix.com/resources719/ssmcag6read

It's Your Moment, Let's Celebrate It!

Share your story @mometrixtestpreparation